Christian
Life Patterns

Christian Life Patterns

THE PSYCHOLOGICAL CHALLENGES AND RELIGIOUS INVITATIONS OF ADULT LIFE

Evelyn Eaton Whitehead
and James D. Whitehead

CROSSROAD • NEW YORK

For our parents,
Evelyn and Homer, Aurea and Ed,
who have generated us
and have engendered this book

1995

The Crosssroad Publishing Company
370 Lexington Avenue, New York, NY 10017

Copyright © 1979 by Evelyn Eaton Whitehead and
James D. Whitehead
Preface to the New Edition © 1992 by Evelyn Eaton Whitehead and
James D. Whitehead

Printed in the United States of America

Library of Congress Cataloging-in-Publication Data

Whitehead, Evelyn Eaton.
    Christian life patterns : the psychological challenges and
religious invitations of adult life / Evelyn Eaton Whitehead and
James D. Whitehead. — New ed.
        p.   cm.
    Includes bibliographical references and index.
    ISBN 0-8245-1154-9 (pbk.)
    1. Christian life—1960–   2. Adulthood.   I. Whitehead, James D.
II. Title.
BV4501.2.W47   1992
248.8′4—dc20
                                            92–11385
                                              CIP

Contents

Preface to the New Edition   6

Introduction   11

1. Change in Adult Life:
   Psychological Patterns and Religious Themes   25

2. Adult Crises: Psychological Structure
   and Religious Meaning   47

3. Intimacy and Mutuality:
   The Challenge of Young Adulthood   71

4. Intimacy and Religious Growth   89

5. The Invitations of the Mid-years   111

6. Religious Generativity   133

7. Development in Mature Age   155

8. To Grow Old Among Christians   173

Conclusion   191

References   205

Index   210

Notes on the Authors   216

Preface
to the New Edition

Love, work, meaning—perennial questions. Now, thirteen years after *Christian Life Patterns* first appeared, these concerns continue to absorb the attention of adults everywhere. Biblical images of journey come alive as believers trace the spiritual significance of their own lives, embracing the hopes and risks that arise in their families and jobs and communities. As the original text of our book becomes available once more, we are eager to acknowledge developments in three important areas that enrich and expand a contemporary spirituality of adult Christian life.

The experience of women became a significant focus of theological and psychological interest through the 1980s. *In Memory of Her: A Feminist Theological Reconstruction of Christian Origins* (Crossroad, 1983), Elisabeth Schüssler Fiorenza's groundbreaking analysis of religion and patriarchy, set the precedent for much subsequent theological reflection. Rosemary Radford Reuther offered a succinct statement of the feminist theological position in *Women-Church: Theology and Practice* (Harper & Row, 1984), along with examples of creative rituals celebrating women's religious experience. Anne Carr's *Transforming Grace: Christian Tradition and Women's Experience* (Harper & Row, 1986) encouraged a recovery of the rich heritage of women's spiritual experience.

Feminist psychologists showed that the challenge posed by developmental questions can be different for women than for men. Take, for instance, an issue raised in close relationships: How can we share deeply with others, in ways that respect and replenish who we really are? The question confronts each of us, but the vulnerabilities of women and men are different. The difficulty for many men revolves around the word *connection.* Men ask, "How can we draw close to other people, in ways that do not threaten our sense of self as independent?" Women more often feel the strain of the word *separation.* They ask, "How can we nourish a sense of personal autonomy, in ways that do not diminish the important connections we have with other people?"

To explain the roots of this fundamental difference, psychologist Nancy Chodorow looked to childrearing practices. Her findings, reported in *The Reproduction of Mothering: Psychoanalysis and the Sociology of Gender* (University of California Press, 1978), serve as the focal point of a significant feminist perspective on gender development. Chodorow notes that in many cultures—ours included—mothers are the primary, sometimes the exclusive, caretakers of young children of either sex. Most often, the first emotionally close relationship that an infant experiences is with the mother. As this primary experience of love develops, a girl child comes gradually to recognize that mother is "not me," even though, as a woman, she is "like me." Her early awareness of self is as *like* mother, as connected with the loved one. The boy child grows into the realization that mother is "not me" but also "not like me." His awareness of self depends on a more profound sense of separation from the loved one. These early differences continue to shape the subsequent experience of women and men, bringing us into adult life with differing—even contradictory— expectations of the rhythms and requirements of closer relationships.

Carol Gilligan's work advances the discussion of gender development and gender differences. Her influential study of moral development among women, *In a Different Voice: Psychological Theory and Women's Development* (Harvard University Press, 1982), demonstrates that women and men often carry different internal models of their experience. These differences, again, influence gender expectations about intimacy.

Intimacy creates bonds between people. Most women feel good about these connections because, in their mental imagery, relationships bring security. Emotional bonds form a supportive net that holds people up and protects them from harm. Although the situation is more complex and conflicted for a woman who has suffered emotional or physical violence from persons close to her, women characteristically approach close relationships with positive expectations.

Men have different internal models. In the imagery of many men bonds imply bondage, so emotional connections are risky. The ties created by close relationships feel more like a trap than a safety net. Characteristically, many men approach close relationships with caution.

Over the past decade, others have built on and amplified this foundational work on gender differences. Carol Tavris and Carole Wade review the research literature in *The Longest War: Sex Differences in Perspective* (Harcourt Brace Jovanovich, 1984). Tavris updates this analysis in *The Mismeasure of Woman: Paradoxes and Perspectives in the Study of Gender* (Simon and Schuster, 1992). Lillian Rubin discusses her own research on women and men, as well as the contributions of other theoretical perspectives, in *Intimate Strangers: Women and Men Together* (Harper & Row, 1983.) In *You Just Don't Understand: Women and Men in Conversation* (Ballentine Books, 1990), Deborah Tannen explores the practical ways that gender differences influence us, as she traces both subtle and significant differences in the communication styles of women and of men. And we look explicitly at issues of gender identity and relationships between men and women in our book, *A Sense of Sexuality: Christian Love and Intimacy* (Image Books/Doubleday, 1990).

Other recent studies trace the patterns of women's development at different life stages. In *Making Connections: The Relational Worlds of Adolescent Girls* (Harvard University Press, 1990), Carol Gilligan and her research colleagues document the subtle socialization efforts directed toward girls, especially during adolescence. Responding to these pressures, girls characteristically "lose their voice" as they move through their teen years. For some women, this begins a lifelong process of distancing themselves from an authentic experience of self. Ruthellen Josselson discusses identity formation in young adult women in *Finding Herself: Pathways to Identity Development in Women* (Jossey-Bass, 1987). Grace Baruch, Rosalind Barnett, and Caryl Rivers report on their examination of the lives of women approaching midlife in *Life Prints: New Patterns of Love and Work for Women* (New American Library, 1983); by including women who have never married and women who are divorced in their study, these authors honor the real diversity of women's experience. And in *Vital Involvement in Old Age* (Norton, 1986), Joan Erikson, Erik Erikson, and Helen Kivnick explore the gains and losses of maturity in the lives of older women and men.

Complementing this deepening understanding of the influence of gender were new probings of the paths and perils of religious development. The often exciting, sometimes hazardous, workings of adult faith became clearer; James Fowler pioneered here with his analysis in *Stages of Faith* (Harper & Row, 1981) and *Becoming Adult, Becoming Christian* (Harper & Row, 1984). Adult Christians today better recognize that virtues survive only by changing. Clinging to the strengths of one stage of life (the innocent docility of the child or the idealistic energy of adolescence) can become a kind of idolatry. Obedience, for example, endures as it expands beyond the young disciple's dependence on religious authority to include a robust, adult attentiveness to God's revelation wherever it is found. Religious fidelity need not make change an enemy: we remain faithful to the journey of faith precisely through canny adjustments, painful letting go, and courageous exploration of new terrain.

These spiritual insights, so ancient that they seemed novel, led Christians to recall another profound dynamic of religious change. Here scripture scholar Walter Brueggemann showed the way. In his reflections on religious change in ancient Israel, begun in *The Prophetic Imagination* (Fortress, 1978) and continued in *Hopeful Imagination* (Fortress, 1986) and *Interpretation and Obedience* (Fortress, 1991), Brueggemann has challenged Christians to recover the healthy, if painful virtue of grief. God continually calls us to *see through* the present with its absorbing demands and constricting "royal" arrangements. In doing this we come to grief: we must let go parts of our life that we thought we could not do without. If letting go is difficult for individual believers, it is most painful for religious institutions. This challenge of institutional purification may be a core religious task of the decade ahead.

A third revelation of the 1980s brought more profound awareness of the impact of our families of origin on the personal journey of faith. Family therapists first opened this avenue of insight. In *The Drama of the Gifted Child* (Basic Books, 1981), Alice Miller sheds light on the wounded child that survives in all of us, still shaping how we love and work. An explosion of research through the 1980s on the dynamics of shame—for example, Gershen Kaufman, *Shame* (Schenkman Books, 1980) as well as Merle Fossum and Marilyn Mason, *Facing Shame: Families in Recovery* (Norton, 1986)—found popular expression in John Bradshaw's influential *Healing the Shame That Binds You* (Health Communications, 1988). Spiritual writers soon recognized the links between the addictions that flow from shame and lives that are spiritually troubled. Gerald May's *Addiction and Grace* (Harper &

Row, 1988) examplifies the rich material now available on this aspect of adult religious growth.

These revelations of the 1980s provide the agenda for the 1990s. Spiritual renewal continues as Christians find ways—through conversion and counseling and communal support—to heal the wounds and addictions that still scar our lives. A movement of small faith communities—some arising amid large active parishes, others thriving apart from institutional affiliation—is stirring in this country and throughout the world. The best of these faith gatherings link strong interpersonal support with shared commitment to justice and social change.

Painful evidence abounds that the need for Christian renewal continues. Poverty and violence expand in our country and elsewhere. Religious institutions balk at the structural purifications that face them—transformations that will yield a richer understanding of sexual fruitfulness, a more honest encouragement of women as leaders, an abandonment of the long-familiar but bankrupt notion of the *laity* as docile, child-like followers.

Amid these signs of stagnation and reversal, the followers of Christ cling to the passion of hope. In our everyday loving and working, we find hints and clues of God's healing presence. Despite—or because of—crises and failures, we remain convinced that the challenge of psychological maturing is finally a religious invitation. We welcome both new and returning readers to share with us the exciting exploration of the adult journeys of faith.

EEW and JDW
February 25, 1992

Introduction

THE NEWS OF ADULT CHANGE

Adulthood takes us by surprise. This is true for many of us today. We can recall approaching our own adulthood with expectations of stability and maturity. Our images were of "settling down" as "grownups," of being—somehow—finished products. For some these images of stability were attractive. They seemed to suggest that, after the tumult of adolescence, we could look forward to a quieter time of life, with a more predictable order and a clearer set of rules. For others this promise of predictability made adulthood seem uninteresting. Surely as "grownups" all the excitement would be gone.

But the experience of adulthood is different. Our sense of stability is often put in question by an awareness of a need for change. Instead of feeling settled, we may be swamped by a sense of uprootedness. Rather than seeing ourselves as "grown-up," we can feel challenged to grow. This realization that adulthood is a time of continuing change and challenge is news. It is not so much news to each of us individually. Those of us who have reached our thirties or our fifties or our seventies can each attest to ways in which we are different now—for better and for worse—than we were at twenty. But most often we have judged that our own experience of change is idiosyncratic—exceptional and uniquely our own. Surely "most adults" live lives of predictable equilibrium, clear about who they are and confident of their adequacy to the tasks that confront them. If my own life does not feel stable or settled, if it seems filled with confusing ambiguities and challenging dilemmas, it must be I who am the exception.

The news, of course, is that this is not the case, that significant personal development should not be unexpected in adulthood, that change is as much a description of the later fifty years of life as of the first twenty-five. This is news because it contradicts the cultural expectations of adulthood that have prevailed over our recent past. The expectations survive not so much as an explicit or well-developed theory, but rather as more subtle and influential presumptions. Many people are sophisticated enough to deny, intellectually, this simplistic stance. But often even these persons find themselves using this expectation of stability to judge themselves and the embarrassing changes of their own adult lives.

This implicit cultural expectation is that adulthood is a relatively stable state, achieved, once and for all, after the unsettled time of childhood and adolescence. Two aspects of this assumption are particularly influential in the cultural expectation: First, adulthood is expected to be relatively stable. The changes of childhood and adolescence, which—though disturbing—are judged to be normal and expectable, have come to an end. Development is over. And, second, this stable state is achieved once and for all. There is an expectation of permanence. In such an expectation, change will be experienced as a scandal, an unanticipated, irregular occurrence and a deterioration from an ideal.

In this understanding, adulthood is seen as a plateau, a leveling off, a settling down. This image of stable adulthood was more adequate to an earlier experience of adult life. Over the history of humankind until this century, few lived beyond fifty years. This brevity of life was accompanied by considerable stability: Life would likely be lived in the same locale, among the same neighbors, performing much the same tasks over one's adult years, in a pattern that would not differ remarkably from the life of one's parents. Over the last century advances in sanitation, nutrition, public health, and medicine have doubled life expectancy in the developed nations. An important effect of this extension of life has been a gradual lengthening of adulthood, or, more precisely, an increase in the number of persons whose lives extend well beyond childhood.

Paralleling the extension of adult life is the extravagant increase in mobility in adulthood. The shift in the United States from a population that was largely agricultural at the turn of the century to one that is almost exclusively urban and suburban today is one indicator of this mobility. Replacing the stability of living in a single locale with the same neighbors and, likely, the same career is the life experience of the average adult in our country, who can be expected to change residence seven times during his or her lifetime. This mobility, which implies significant adjustments regarding one's friendships and lifework, unmasks a deception lingering in our language about adult life. This is the use of a single word (such as "wife," "husband," "parent," or "priest") to describe a lifelong choice and commitment. Fidelity to one's marriage or vocational commitment does not mean clinging to a single, unchanging understanding (formed in one's twenties) but faithfully responding to the different demands and invitations hidden in this single life as it is lived out over half a century. A striking instance of this necessary pluralism of response required within a single life is the shift in the length and structure of marriage. Today a couple can expect almost twenty years of life together after the last child has left home. A century ago this stage of married life, a period which requires definite adjustment and growth, simply did not exist.

These changes in length and shape have brought the terrain of adult life into sharper focus. It is not a plateau but a rugged, more interesting landscape. Over the past few decades systematic attempts have begun to map this terrain. Developmental psychologists and others are engaged in the effort to understand what, in fact, does go on in adulthood, what is the experience of persons over the fifty-year expanse from their thirties into their seventies and eighties. Information that collects from these investigations reinforces the personal experience of adulthood as a time of marked variation and challenges the earlier image of adulthood as a time of stability unaffected (at least ideally) by change. What is emerging is a new understanding of adulthood, not as a somewhat static period of relative stability but as a dynamic series of expectable changes that make up a normal sequence of adult development. Maturity appears now less a question of fidelity to expectations learned in early adult life and more one of effective adaptation to the different and often surprising challenges that arise during the five or six decades of one's adult life.

This book will focus on two aspects of this radical change in the expectations about adult life and maturity. We will review and expand perspectives from developmental psychology on adult growth and its specific challenges and tasks. We will also explore some of the religious meanings and potential in the contemporary experience of adult life. Mindful that most of our Christian convictions and interpretations of maturity were elaborated during those centuries in which adulthood was a brief and relatively stable experience, we will suggest religious responses to the changes in adult life that are both psychologically informed and thoroughly Christian.

GROWTH AS DEVELOPMENT

A central challenge of adult life concerns the understanding and management of change. Change threatens past accomplishments; it disrupts stability. Change often feels like loss, failure, or, for the Christian, sin. In this book we will examine adult change in terms of development. The idea of development adds to the notion of change at least two features: pattern, or order; and direction, or sequence. Among the social sciences, developmental psychology has emerged as a discipline particularly concerned with understanding the patterns and directions of change throughout the life-span. The developmental psychologist's interest in adult change, then, is not focused on the unique or idiosyncratic events in adult living but on the general patterns of growth and development that, common to many adults, are an expectable part of adult life.

Development may also include the notion of improvement. To call a change a development is to suggest that the later stages of the process both depend upon and are in some sense "better" than the earlier, that they are a fulfillment or a completion of what has gone before. While not all students of adulthood are explicit in their use of development in the sense of completion, this meaning is clearly part of the developmental understanding of Erik Erikson, whose work provides a framework for our discussion.

RELIGIOUS IMAGES OF GROWTH

Lying behind Erikson's notion of development, which will be examined in detail in the next chapter, are the different metaphors of change and development in the Western cultural and religious tradition. Central among these metaphors is that of agricultural growth. Sowing and harvesting are frequent images in the Old and New Testaments for religious growth. Such natural unfolding and coming to maturity is, for the believer, both originally structured and existentially assisted by God: Human efforts of sowing and cultivating are more than complemented by God, who gives the increase. In the Book of Genesis (26:12) Isaac reaps a hundredfold; Paul reminds his followers that although he planted and Apollos watered, "God gave the growth" (1 Cor. 3:6).

This agricultural metaphor reveals a profound optimism—things are inclined to grow; both plants and human persons have the potential to develop in ways that are healthy and to become fruitful. If the believer acknowledges the intervention of God in this process, it is nonetheless a process of natural development.

The metaphor of natural growth has likewise been invoked beyond the Western tradition. The Chinese scholar Mencius, writing about 300 B.C., turned to this image to argue the natural goodness of human development. In one of his most celebrated passages he likens human growth to that of the once well-forested Mount Niu. This mountain has lost its luxuriant growth not of its own accord but because of environmental abuse; ravaged by men's axes, it continues its struggle to grow. Human development is similarly frustrated. Although the times have caused much human failure and stunted growth, at certain privileged moments ("in the still air of the early morning") a person can perceive "those desires and aversions which are proper to the human person" (book 6A, chap. 8).[1] Earlier in his writing (book 2A, chap. 2) Mencius turned to the image of developing corn to describe human growth. The farmer may respond to the maturing corn in three ways: neglecting it by providing no cultivation or care; fostering and nourishing its growth; or interfering and trying to force it to grow. Mencius gives an example of this third response: "A man of Sung was grieved that his growing corn was not longer, so he pulled it up. He then returned home, looking very stupid and said to his people, 'I am tired today; I have been helping the corn to grow.' His son ran to look at it and found the corn all withered."

The American psychologist Robert White (1975) describes the

1. For full bibliographic information see list of References at the back of the book.

development of children in imagery reminiscent of Mencius. A person who would foster the growth of a child is like a farmer who "does not poke at the seed in order to make it sprout more quickly, nor does he seize the shoot when it breaks ground and try to pull open the first leaves by hand" (p. 368).

Countering the optimism of this metaphor of natural development is a profound conviction within Christianity that religious growth is growth *against nature*. St. Paul adds to the image of the natural growth of the olive tree (signifying Israel, the people of God) the notion of grafting. Gentiles converted to Christ and brought into the saving community are likened to wild olive shoots "grafted, contrary to nature, into a cultivated olive tree" (Rom. 11:24). This grafting, the gracious activity of God, points both to the "unnaturalness" of religious growth and its giftedness. More broadly, religious growth must be understood in the light of both grace and sin.

The role of grace in human development points to the giftedness of life and the unexpectedness of its healings and increases. The surprising increases and recoveries in growth stand in opposition to what the believer expected to happen. They are, to this extent, "unnatural." Christians have long been divided over how this gracious intervention and assistance of God occurs— whether from within, by fostering a person's natural inclination to maturity, or from without "fallen nature" and in opposition to the human inclination to evil and sin. These opposing interpretations in Christianity of the relationship of natural growth and gracious development are also reflected in a Christian's posture toward "the world." A Christian antagonism against the world finds it a hostile and alien place. Such a Christian finds no home here and learns to distrust natural processes of growth and the allure of worldly effectiveness and development. Another view within Christian experience has more optimistically seen the world as still very much God's creation, as at bottom a lovely if flawed place to live. This view identifies the broken and unredeemed aspects of nature and the world with these elements within the believer. Sharing this brokenness, both the human person and the natural world struggle toward and await healing.

The present authors, influenced by the traditional Catholic optimism about the intimate relation and even potential partnership[2] of nature and grace, will pursue an interpretation of adult development in which God's grace can be discovered at work within the structure of psychosocial development. The psychological challenges, crises, and tasks of human development present opportunities and invitations that a believer can recognize as graceful. These may appear as unanticipated failure, as the discovery of a personal strength, or as the bitter experience of one's own sinfulness. Yet "believers" describes those who, responding to and integrating these experiences into their adult lives, find themselves gifted with an unexpected growth or blessed with a reconciliation of which they seemed incapable. Growth for such persons is both natural development and a surprisingly graceful event.

Grace, to be sure, alters nature. Religious faith can alter the expectable schedule of human development, either extending or compressing it. Abraham and Sarah's conception of Isaac at an advanced age instances the religious extension of creativity and generativity. The Roman Catholic liturgy for St. Stanislaus, who died as a young man, attests to a precocious maturity: "Being perfected in a short time, he fulfilled long years" (Wisdom 4:13). This compression of maturity into a relatively short period of growth pertains pre-eminently for the Christian to Jesus Christ, whose adult growth was truncated according to one schedule, yet fulfilled according to another, more mysterious, schedule.

If grace can alter, either to change or to deepen the patterns of human growth, sin can shatter and atrophy them. If the optimism of creation and the garden stand at the beginning of the Christian story, sin and the frustration of nature are its second chapter. Tragedy, absurdity, and personal failure break the expectable patterns of human development. Sin, as the chosen activity of the human person and community, joins these as disruptive of life and growth.

This book is not specifically about sin, though we include a discussion of the relation of sin and maturity in the chapter which follows. In our consideration of the schedule and dynamic of adult development, however, we are interested in crises, personal

2. The Catholic theologian Karl Rahner (1968) describes the relationship of nature and grace in these terms: "Nature is rather that reality which the divine self-communication creatively posits for itself as *its possible partner* in such a way that in relation to it that communication does and can remain what it is: a free and loving favor" (p. 417; our emphasis).

failure, and loss. These crises and failures that intersect adult living invite the Christian into the mystery of Christ's cross, death, and resurrection. We will turn frequently to such crises and failures (sinful or not) to explore both their death-to-life dynamic and the reconciliation required as one negotiates the passages of adult life.

THE WAY OF GROWTH:
HEALTH AND HOLINESS

The Christian Gospels and Freudian theory agree that effective adult living consists in the abilities to love well and work well. These abilities, understood in their most profound sense, allow the self-expression and self-transcendence necessary for effective engagement with others and one's social world.

Controversy abounds concerning more specific definitions of personal maturity. The "mental health" research approach (Jahoda, 1959) has delineated a range of characteristics of the healthy person. Erikson (IYC, p. 92)[3] summarizes these in three general features: active mastery of the environment, unity of the personality, and perceiving the world and oneself correctly. Active mastery of the environment includes one's ability to work and play, but also one's relationship to diet, exercise, and use of time. Such mastery is dependent on the unity of the personality—awareness of and relative comfort with one's feelings and convictions, as well as consonance between one's inner world and external behavior. The ability to perceive the world and self correctly entails a recognition of the boundaries between self and other and the ability to cross these boundaries, not to dominate or absorb but to share something of oneself and allow oneself to be reached. Coming full circle, such perception facilitates mastery of the environment—the ability to invest oneself in the world and contribute to its growth.

A major gain in recent years has been the recognition that such health occurs along a continuum. Health and illness are not rigidly exclusive categories; we are, all of us, part healthy and part ill, changing in the maturity of our responses to life.

3. See list of References for a key to the abbreviations used in citing Erikson's work.

The dynamic of healthy growth through adulthood has been brought into sharper relief in the past several decades because of the work of such pioneering developmental psychologists as Charlotte Buhler, Robert Havighurst, and Bernice Neugarten. More recently a number of studies of adult maturation have contributed to our working knowledge of this lengthy and complex part of life. The Grant Study of Harvard University students, a longitudinal effort begun in 1937, is summarized and interpreted by George Vaillant in *Adaptation to Life* (1977). A Yale study of a smaller group of men over a shorter period is reported in Daniel Levinson's *The Seasons of a Man's Life* (1978). In her popular work *Passages* (1976) Gail Sheehy presents elements from Levinson's and others' research in a simplified and often insightful fashion. A less biographical, cross-sectional study of the patterns of response to adult change is provided by Marjorie Fiske Lowenthal and her colleagues in *Four Stages of Life* (1976). Healthy adulthood in these studies is understood not in terms of an absence of problems but as a way of reacting to them. That is, health is not so much a state to be achieved; it is, rather, an effective mode of adaption to the challenges of life.

The theoretical perspective of Erik Erikson reflects this orientation. In *Identity: Youth and Crisis* he comments, "I shall present human growth from the point of view of the conflicts, inner and outer, which the vital personality weathers, re-emerging from each crisis with an increased sense of inner unity, with an increase of good judgment, and an increase in the capacity 'to do well' according to his own standards and to the standards of those who are significant to him" (pp. 91–92). Such crises often appear in the guise of illness, with symptoms of disorientation, confusion, and depression. With Vaillant (p. 369) we suggest that these symptoms are similar to the pus around an infection or the swelling around a fracture. They represent efforts of the organism to deal with conflict and to heal an inner distress. In such instances growth and health are facilitated not by attacking these symptoms but by allowing them to achieve their healing intent. Such an orientation is not to deny the reality of the distress and its features of loss and even sin. But it recognizes that such crises are the developmental challenges in response to which we grow. Health—

and holiness—is realized not in the avoidance of such crises but in an effective response and adaptation to them.[4]

HOLINESS:
HAZARDOUS TO YOUR HEALTH?

There is a strong tradition in the Christian and Jewish experience that holiness is dangerous and potentially destructive. Moses learned that seeing the face of Yahweh—too direct an encounter with holiness—would cause his death (Ex. 33). A follower of the ark of the covenant on its way to Jerusalem drew too close to this repository of God's holiness and was struck dead (2 Sam. 6:6–7). In Christian spirituality, growth in holiness has often been interpreted as growth at the expense of physical health. Even Josef Goldbrunner, whose influential book *Holiness Is Wholeness* (1964) argued against a dichotomy of natural health and holiness, felt compelled to admit: "Spiritual life is a strain on our health" (p. 2). Many of the saints of the Christian Church seemed to attain to holiness despite or even because of peculiar and "unhealthy" characteristics.

The crucial question here for the contemporary Christian is the relationship of health and holiness, or, more fundamentally, of nature and grace. Are these two utterly different orders of growth? Are nature and grace simply antagonistic, or is there a possibility of partnership? If "natural" translates as the tendency of a person to overindulge, to be hateful and manipulative of others, then spiritual growth and maturity are achieved by going against nature. If, however, overindulgence and other destructive behaviors are interpreted as unnatural—as aberrations, compensations, and failures to grow according to natural, healthy proclivities, then Christian growth and psychosocial maturation may be seen as more complementary than antagonistic.

In the Christian tradition holiness has often been located at the developmental extremes. It is equated either with childhood, met-

4. Vaillant quotes the conclusion of another longitudinal study, conducted by Frank Barron at the University of California, as summarizing the motif of his own research: "The conclusion to which the assessment study has come is that psychopathology is always with us and *soundness is a way of reacting to problems, not an absence of them*" (pp. 2–3; our emphasis).

aphorical or real, or with perfect and final maturity. In this book we trace the development of holiness as it occurs over the life-span. Religious growth will be charted in terms of an adult's maturing sense of identity (discipleship), the ability to love and give of oneself (charity), and the capacity for responsible care (stewardship). Intervening throughout this maturing process will be a variety of developmental crises, scheduled and unscheduled opportunities for growth. Such growth, psychological and religious, must be achieved in response to loss and failure; it necessitates a reintegration and reconciliation of the adult with oneself and with the community.

Holiness, like health, is ultimately success at living. This does not mean attaining some ideal norm of either maturity or sanctity. It does not mean avoiding problems or even sin. Health and holiness also do not have to "look good." Vaillant repeatedly observes that the healthiest subjects of his study displayed many immature reactions and knew many serious failures and sufferings. Their health consisted in their adaptation to these losses and challenges in such a way that they could love and work effectively.

Grace is at work within the structure of adult growth and the crises that mark its advance. A maturing Christian is one whose responses to the challenges and invitations of life effect the kind of loving and working that Jesus and his Church have modeled. An ultimate criterion of religious maturity is neither good intentions nor a well-rounded personality. It is, instead, the ability to be loving and generative, and to discover within the unexpected turns and crosses of adult life a meaning that is, at bottom, a gift.

PERSONAL EXPERIENCE: PARTNER IN THE CONVERSATION

In this book we explore the patterns of contemporary adult growth at two levels—the expectable psychological challenges that an adult encounters and the often disguised religious invitations that are present within these challenges. These patterns suggest the shape of adult maturation as well as the schedule of the developmental tasks, psychological and religious, that await a growing person. The theoretical work of Erik Erikson provides the framework for our discussion. At the psychological level this is supplemented by the findings and interpretations of others active in the study of adulthood, particularly the work of Neugarten, Vaillant, Levinson, Lowenthal, and Sennett. Religiously, we turn to the Scriptures for the images that ground a Christian understanding of adult life. Love, power, reconciliation, grace, death, resurrection —these themes recur to illumine and challenge the psychological categories of growth.

Ours is a book about adult religious growth for adults who are growing religiously. Thus, we invite the reader to participate in its conversation. Theology and psychology are partners in our coming discussion. But there is a third perspective that is critical as well— the personal experience of adult growth. One's life is itself an important source of information on religious adulthood. It has been a time of change and of stability, of crisis and of development, of loss and of gain, of sin and of grace. We invite the recovery of these experiences in order that they may be brought to new awareness. They serve an active purpose here, to critique and to confirm the observations that arise from other religious and psychological sources.

To facilitate this three-way conversation, we will suggest several reflective exercises in the course of our discussion of adult growth. These exercises are an invitation to self-exploration, to a critical attending to one's own life experience. Some initial remarks may be helpful. Religious persons are sometimes reluctant to engage in exercises of this kind. There is a scent of narcissism here: such direct attention to myself when I could be serving God and neighbor! Yet as religious persons we value the self-knowledge that comes in introspection and know the perils of the unreflective life. The Christian believes in God's abiding presence; an inner reflection can be expected to reveal God within. This is especially so when we look back to an experience too dense or disruptive to fathom at the time it occurred. In the stillness of a later reflection the usually invisible, though active, presence of God may be sighted.

But this kind of recollection requires both method and skill. Systematic steps help us return carefully and concretely to experiences that are heavy with feeling and meaning, that remain half-buried in our past. There are three general suggestions that can be made.

The first suggestion is that it is important to find a quiet environment, one in which time and space allow the recollection to occur at an unhurried pace. This means selecting a place that is congenial, where one is not likely to be interrupted, and a time when one is not too tired or distracted.

A second suggestion is that these exercises be pursued in community. This means, simply, that the reflection or the resulting insight be shared with some others who care. This feature of the exercise provides for two things: an opportunity to deepen the realization of the reflection by disclosing it to another, and a protective environment in which to approach a potentially dangerous or frightening part of one's inner life. To return to a powerful event of my past is often to release unknown or unanticipated feelings. Whether these be positive or negative, it is important that they emerge in a context of caring adults.

The third suggestion is that the reflection be concrete rather than vague or general. In both the exercise and in the sharing that may follow, it is most helpful to be able to speak concretely (Egan, 1975)—to name the actual events, feelings, and convictions as I become aware of them. Such concreteness often is aided by recording the reflection in some fashion, whether in a personal journal (Progoff, 1975) or through the use of a symbol, chart, or picture.

The chapters ahead can, of course, be read on their own merit. It is our conviction, however, that their value will be enhanced through participation in the several reflective exercises we suggest along the way. These can provide for the reader a personal perspective from which to engage and evaluate the authors' interpretation of religious growth in adulthood. Again, we invite you to the conversation.

ONE

Change in Adult Life: Psychological Patterns and Religious Themes

We invite you to return to a recent experience of transition or change in your own life. Recall the last several months, the last few years. What events stand out for you now as having been points of transition? Don't force yourself to respond to the question; just raise it and wait to see what comes to mind. Spend some time in this recollection.

Now, from among these memories, select one experience that strikes you as having had some effect, positive or negative, on who you are now. This need not be the most significant experience—rather a memory that catches your attention today. In the quiet of this reflective mood, return to the experience to learn from it, to have it disclose something of itself that was too full or too forbidding to be grasped fully at the time. The return should be gradual. First recall the event itself, then something of its context: Who was involved in it with you? How did the experience come to conclusion? As you recall the facts of the experience, allow the return of some of the feelings that accompany it. It is important to remain responsible to oneself in the exercise, allowing the reflection to reach the depth that is appropriate for this time and this situation. The exercise is not meant as a therapeutic tool but as an experiential one. Its intent is to put you in touch with the texture of adult change in your own life. Spend enough time with the experience to allow it to become real again to you.

Now consider the following questions. Their goal is to assist in your own reflection. To the extent that they do this, spend time with them. To the extent that they seem intrusive or distracting, just set them aside.

What did this experience mean to you at the time? What did it say to you then about yourself or your life?

What does it mean to you now? Has your evaluation of it changed since its occurrence?

Are there ways in which this experience still affects your life today?

Change pervades and shapes our contemporary lives. Social change is a dominant cultural theme. It is one of the "images" (Boulding, 1956) of contemporary American society—a symbol that expresses our sense of how things are, an accepted description of what our world is like. Personal change is an even more prevalent theme. Our own lives are testimony to its challenges. And our culture offers us magazines, merchandize, machines, medicines—all designed to help us "cope with change." We set out here to examine the dynamic of personal change: the ways in which it is experienced over the course of adult life and the ways in which it can be understood, religiously and psychologically.

PSYCHOLOGY AND PERSONAL CHANGE

Who am I?
Who am I with?
What should I do?
What does it all mean?
These questions can be asked at several levels. They are, at one level, "small talk," the substance of the incidental conversations we have with people in a variety of casual situations. When asked in the anguish of personal crisis, however, these can be questions of deep individual significance. They are the serious human questions dealt with in the great literature of every culture. And they are religious questions as well. They are asked and answered in sermons and catechisms. Even those who find sermon and catechism answers too often unsatisfying may attest to the religious overtones of the questions themselves.

These are the perennial questions of human experience, never fully resolved or finally answered, returned to at all the important points in one's life. And so they are of interest to the psychologist as well. These questions underscore the issues that are central to psychological maturity. One's ability to respond, in the variety of situations in which the questions arise, is an index of one's psychological strength. They also point to resources of the personality, capacities that are called out, tested and strengthened as the individual resolves the challenge that each question provokes.

For the psychologist the questions are essentially related. To ask any one of them at a serious level raises all the others. Thus an experience of a failure or a defeat in my work (What can I do?) can leave me confused about my self (Who am I?). New information which changes my response to any one of these questions will lead me to reformulate my answer to the others. An experience of being loved deeply (Who am I with?) can bring me to a new understanding of what my life is about (What does it all mean?).

Interrelated as these questions are, however, developmental psychologists suggest that there is a pattern in the way in which they are experienced over the life-span. During adolescence the question "Who am I?" is paramount. It is not only in adolescence that the question is raised. As we have said, the question is asked anew at each point of important change throughout life. In adolescence, however, it is central. The issue of identity functions as a prism through which much else in the young person's life is refracted. And the success of the identity resolution the adolescent reaches will condition all later efforts to come to terms with "who I am." During the mature years of late adulthood "What does it all mean?" becomes the question of particular concern. The significance of my own life, its meaning to me, and its place in the larger scheme of things—these are not issues that appear for the first time in later adulthood, but they appear then with special poignancy. During the long period of early and middle adulthood the remaining questions are particularly relevant. Who am I with; and how am I with people? These issues of intimacy and mutuality arise for the young adult around experiences of friendship and love, of co-operation and competition. In the mid-years, issues of power and morality become prominent and the questions "What can I do?" "What should I do?" become a focus of special concern.

THE DEVELOPMENTAL PERSPECTIVE
OF ERIK ERIKSON

These questions parallel the issues of adult development as understood by Erik Erikson. More strongly than some observers of adult change, Erikson stresses the developmental character of much in adult experience. There are several points central to Erikson's understanding that are, increasingly, shared by other students of adult life. We will note these here, and then turn our focus to the stages of adult development.

1. There is available to each person a range of psychological strengths and resources. These resources are based in the genetic make-up of the human species and thus, in one sense, "given" for each individual from conception. At the start of life these strengths exist in potential. Only gradually over the course of one's life are these resources realized as consistent characteristics of the personality. The process of the unfolding of the personality does not only occur in infancy or through adolescence but continues over the entire life-span. There are, in fact, aspects of the personality which are developed into consistent personal strengths only in the mature years.

2. There is a pattern to be seen in this unfolding, a normal, expectable sequence to the process through which the resources of the personality are called forth. Many particulars of the process and the events that occasion it will differ from person to person. And there are variations in timing and intensity that result from cultural factors as well. But an underlying similarity will be seen in both the dynamics of the process and the basic psychological concern which initiates it. Erikson describes this sequence in terms of his now-classic epigenetic model of psychological development. The processes are developmental, for Erikson, in that they effect "a progression through time of a differentiation of parts" (CS, p. 271).

3. The emergence of each new psychological resource or strength marks a critical time for the individual, a decisive moment in personal development. At a point in an individual's life a particular concern becomes central. This concern raises a significant question to the person, challenges the current state of one's life and one's level of self-understanding. The resolution of this challenge will require a judgment, a choice, a decisive action that will carry important implications for what follows in one's life. As a result of this encounter with myself, I will be different—whether I accept the challenge and move through it to a more confident possession of personality strengths or back away from the challenge and refuse (from fear or lack of support) to face the question it raises about myself.

For some, this critical time may be experienced as a "crisis" in the colloquial sense, as precipitating a breakdown. For most, however, these crucial adult experiences will not be accompanied by serious emotional deterioration. But the experience will be critical for all, marking a turning point in life and giving decisive shape to one's subsequent development. As Erikson states, "Crisis is used here in a developmental sense to connote not a threat of catastrophe, but a turning point, a crucial period of increased vulnerability and heightened potential" (IYC, p. 96).

4. The self-confrontation provoked by each of these developmental challenges will put the individual in contact with contradictory impulses and with both positive and negative aspects of the personality. The resolution that Erikson suggests is not the unwavering suppression of the negative impulse nor an aggressive dominance by the positive. At any stage, maturity is achieved through a blending of these ambiguous dimensions in a "favorable ratio," a personally appropriate synthesis that is true to one's history and personality. Such a synthesis produces a consistent psychological strength that fits into and completes the character of the individual.

With these elements of Erikson's perspective as background, we turn now to an examination of adulthood.

CRITICAL STAGES OF ADULT LIFE

At several points over the course of the adult life-span a person moves into a period of special developmental importance. At each of these stages there is a decisive encounter of the person with his or her environment. This encounter is brought on in part by changes within the individual that bring the person to a new readiness for development. This readiness is reinforced by factors in the social environment (increased responsibilities and new expectations) that make their own demands for change.

This meeting of personal readiness and social expectation issues in a critical time in the life of the person. An underlying question emerges. In young adulthood it is the question of how one is to be close to other people. In the mid-years it is a question of the breadth and direction of one's effective concern for the world. In the mature years of late adulthood it is the question of finding or giving meaning to one's own life. The adult experiences an opposition between the invitations and demands of this emerging question and the somewhat established order of one's current life. For the young adult this opposition is between newly evoked impulses toward both *intimacy* and isolation. On the one hand, the person is stirred by the hope of discovering a loved partner with whom to share life, work, and love in ways that are mutually satisfying and enriching. Equally the young adult is drawn to protect and defend the sense of independent selfhood that has been but recently achieved. In middle adulthood the opposition is between the impulse to broaden the scope of one's concern to include effective involvement in an expanding social network and the impulse to focus one's efforts and energies upon oneself and a narrow circle of intimates. Both these impulses, toward *generative engagement* and toward self-centered concern, are activated by the encounter between self and society in one's middle age. In late adulthood the encounter between self and society evokes new impulses. There is the turn toward self-assessment that can lead to an acceptance of one's life as meaningful and appropriate. There is, equally, the tendency to defend against the diminishments of aging and the inevitability of death. Here the struggle is between the movement toward *personal integrity* and the opposing movement toward despair.

The crisis of which Erikson speaks is the challenge with which the person is faced as he or she experiences these opposing impulses. This is a decisive period in personal development, a critical time in one's life. Some resolution must be reached. The person may decide not to face this new challenge, not to deal with the new questions raised, but rather to remain with the resolution of an earlier stage. But there is no reprieve. To choose not to face a new developmental challenge is to choose not stasis but stagnation. The "strengths" of earlier stages of development remain so only as they are tested and transformed at later stages. Without this subsequent transformation, earlier strengths atrophy into defended or immature responses. If not modified through the challenges of intimacy and generativity, the appropriately delimited identity of the adolescent may harden into the middle-aged "self-made man."

Even when the developmental challenge is faced rather than avoided, the elements of crisis remain. There is still a demand for personal decision. One must choose, among the diverse and often contradictory impulses newly released in one's personality, those which shall prevail. Will intimacy or isolation dominate my stance toward others? Will my personal power be focused chiefly on myself or upon the larger world? Will wisdom or despair characterize my mature years? One's response cannot be a simple either-or. One is not *either* intimate with others *or* isolated from them. One is both.

This resolution of each critical challenge (What shall I do about being close to people? What shall I do about focusing my productive energy and concern? What shall I do about understanding the meaning of my life?) is achieved in some combination of the "positively" directed and "negatively" directed impulses that are evoked by the question itself. A developmentally favorable combination—one which continues the processes of personal expansion and differentiation—is one in which the positive impulses are in balance over the negative ones. But both positive and negative impulses remain. A mature stance toward other people includes the impulse to selectivity and solitude. The generative adult can care for himself or herself as well as for others. And psychological wisdom is not achieved in old age by the denial of the real diminishments of aging and death. The particulars of this favorable balance of maturity will differ from culture to culture, among subcultures, and between individuals. The degree of positive over negative, the quality and flexibility of the synthesis, the situations that call upon these resources or test their balance—all these will differ according to individual and cultural variations.

Through the effort to face and resolve each of these critical issues one comes into full and confident possession of personal resources available only intermittently or impulsively before. These essential strengths become habitual attitudes and consistent behavior in one's character. Erikson speaks of these inherent strengths, evoked and tested in the developmental challenges of adulthood and embodied in the mature character, as virtues (IR, p. 112). Through the developmental challenge of young adulthood the opposing impulses of intimacy and isolation can be transformed into a capacity for mutual devotion, into the consistent strength of *love*. In middle age the critical opposition between one's generative and one's self-centered impulses can be overcome as one develops a personally appropriate style of *care*. And the crisis of personal significance in the late adult years can find its resolution in a synthesis of meaning and despair that results in *wisdom*. Love, care, and wisdom are resources of the personality that are released only over the span of the adult years. These strengths, essential for the individual and for society, are the fruit of the individual's struggle to meet the challenge of adult growth. They are the virtues of adult maturity.

Intimacy, generativity, and integrity are, then, the key psychological issues of adulthood. Each term is used by Erikson, alternately, to designate (1) a particular challenge ("nuclear conflict" [CS, p. 270]) which the adult will face, (2) more broadly, the developmental stage or period during which the adult is dealing primarily with this challenge, and (3) the resources of personality ("ego strengths" [IR, p. 112]) that are evoked and strengthened as the individual deals with this challenge during its critical period of developmental ascendency. In this volume we use these three concepts to organize our discussion of adulthood as a time of psychological growth and continuing religious development.

As stages of adult development intimacy, generativity, and integrity are umbrella categories under which a variety of particular events are gathered. Each refers not simply to an incident but to a set of personal issues that becomes dominant at a particular point in one's adulthood. At the time of its developmental prominence each set of concerns permeates one's life. For the young adult intimacy is not a question limited to romance. It is an issue at work, among peers, in one's attitude toward oneself. For the middle-aged adult, generativity questions arise within one's family, at one's job, in one's civic responsibilities. The senior adult confronts questions of personal meaning in terms of both love and work, of the past and the present. In its own developmental time, each "set" of concerns serves as a psychological screen through which one's broader experience is filtered. For each of us there may be a certain event which highlights our own struggle with a particular developmental issue. For me, the decision to accept a new job may set off deeper questions of my own productive involvement in society. For you, the marriage of your youngest child may raise new questions of your relationship with your children and their future. For one person, a divorce in middle age may precipitate an emotional breakdown and a subsequent retreat into self-absorption. For another, it may lead to a time of questioning from which the individual emerges even stronger. Each of these is an instance of a critical event in which the broader challenge of generativity is crystallized in personal experience. Each may set off a "crisis" of generativity, issuing in a period of personal reassessment. For some, this will be a period of conflict, stress, and disorientation. For many, however, the developmental struggle of this period will not manifest itself as a "crisis" in this sense. But it will remain, in Erikson's more technical sense, a crisis: "a critical step—critical being a characteristic of turning points, of moments of decision between progress and regression, integration and retardation" (CS, pp. 270–71).

It is possible, and even useful, to focus separately on these stages of adult development in order to explore more thoroughly their psychological and religious potential. We must remember, however, that adulthood—indeed, life—is seldom experienced in intervals that coincide neatly with the logic of theories. Our own lives are experienced as movement and, most often, as messy. In the discussion that follows we shall be concerned with the larger shape and direction of life as well as its stages.

CHRISTIANITY AND PERSONAL CHANGE

CONVERSION AND DEVELOPMENT

The personal change of central concern in Christianity, from its inception, has been conversion and radical transformation (*metanoia*). The initial chapter of the earliest Gospel announces the need for such change: "John the baptizer appeared in the wilderness, preaching a baptism of repentance [*metanoia*] for the forgiveness of sins" (Mark 1:4). Jesus' first public announcement on beginning his career called for total conversion: "The time is fulfilled, and the kingdom of God is at hand; repent, and believe in the gospel" (Mark 1:15). This change, at the heart of the Christian gospel, refers not to improvement or development but to a transformation of life. The images are stark and powerful: death to sin in order to live in God; conversion from the status of slave to that of son and heir; transformation from darkness to light and from the way of the flesh to the way of the spirit.

The controlling metaphor of Christian transformation is that of rebirth. Dying to one's former life and sinfulness, a Christian is born again, baptized into a new order of reality and "a new creation" (2 Cor. 5:17). Despite its central importance, an imbalance can result from an exclusive focus on this image. It can lead to an interpretation of life in dualistic terms: One is either a slave or free, either saved or a sinner. Such sharp delineation of states of being may give greater impact to preaching, but it tends to neglect the areas of twilight and semiliberation that mark Christian experience in adulthood.

When this powerful image of rebirth is joined to that of command, a metaphor of great importance in Protestant theology (Hauerwas, 1975), Christian life can be understood in nondevelopmental terms. The metaphor of command expresses the conviction that Christian life consists in faithful obedience to God's commands. Since these have no discernible relationship to any natural patterns of human growth, "the object of the moral life is not to grow but to be repeatedly ready to obey each new command" (p. 2).[1] The image of rebirth focuses not on growth but on the transition from death to life; the metaphor of command focuses on the discontinuous moments of the person's response to God. Neither metaphor addresses—in fact, each of them obscures—the challenge of religious *development*: how an adult believer is to become better, that is, more virtuous and consistent, in responding constructively to the active and ongoing presence of God in human life.

Religious development concerns life after conversion. But "religious development" has been a suspect category among many religious thinkers. Does not concern for such development always imply some human effort at self-justification? Is not such interest in the patterns of religious growth really a faithless effort to control one's life with God? The goal of religious development is sanctification. But, as Karl Barth would argue, such development is always exclusively God's work; it is thus necessarily "inaccessible and concealed."[2] Such an orientation reflects the deeply Protestant concern to safeguard the agency and sovereignty of God. Its effect, however, can be to interpret Christian adulthood exclusively in terms of the discontinuous moments of one's obedience to God's commands. The human person is necessarily passive in

1. Hauerwas is here criticizing this orientation to the moral life, as he prepares to outline his understanding of an ethics of character.
2. Karl Barth, *Church Dogmatics*, quoted in Hauerwas, p. 170.

this relationship, and these moments lack any discernible pattern or nexus with natural human development.

An alternate understanding of Christian life after conversion encourages the active participation of believers in their own religious development. Such a view builds on the long tradition of religious life and asceticism in Christianity. Asceticism here refers to those human efforts to discern and to respond in a systematic way to God's active presence in the world. The religious development which is the goal of such asceticism need not be understood as an effort at self-justification; it can be seen rather as growth in one's ability to discern patterns of God's presence within human life and to respond in an increasingly open way to this presence.

If the metaphor of command suggests the passivity of adult life, the image of rebirth may suggest a new but static stage of life where the saved or chosen abide. The roots of such a conception of adult life can be found in the vocabulary of the New Testament. St. Paul's description of the "mature" believer as *teleios* (completed, perfect) and Jerome's Latin translation of this as *perfectus* supported the Greek ideal of manhood as a plateau or estate.[3] Paul himself, in his letter to the Philippians, challenges this static view of Christian adulthood as he assures his readers: "Not that I have already obtained this [resurrection with Christ] or am already perfect; but I press on to make it my own, because Christ Jesus has made me his own" (3:12–15). And as Paul presses on, he urges those in the community who are mature (*teleioi*) to do likewise.

The ambiguity between being mature and being called still to grow is increased by the passage in the letter to the Ephesians[4] which describes the goal of Christian growth—". . . until we all attain . . . to mature manhood, to the measure of the stature of the fulness of Christ" (4:13). Here it is suggested that it is Christ alone who is mature and an adult; Christian growth is then growth *toward* adulthood rather than *in* adulthood. William Bouwsma (1976), in arguing for an understanding of Christian adulthood which includes the notion of development and process,

3. William Bouwsma distinguishes the Greek ideal of "manhood" from the Christian ideal of "adulthood" in his "Christian Adulthood" (1976).

4. Although it is the consensus of current biblical scholarship that this letter was not written by Paul himself, it nonetheless has enjoyed an important position in the "Pauline writings."

quotes Calvin's commentary on this passage in Ephesians: "After being born in Christ, we ought to grow so as not to be children in understanding. . . . although we have not arrived at *man's estate*, we are at any rate *older boys*" (p. 81).[5] Not only is the vocabulary of maturation thoroughly chauvinist (manhood, older boys), but Christian development in such a framework is necessarily interpreted as adolescent growth; adulthood, "man's estate," is a plateau of perfection attained exclusively by Jesus Christ.[6]

If the Pauline writings contribute to this static interpretation of Christian adulthood, they are also filled with an insistence on growth and the maturing struggle. Not only does Paul stress the need to "press on," but he recognizes the role of death and suffering as part of the dynamic of this pressing on (2 Cor. 4:12). Christian maturity, rather than a plateau of perfection, involves an unsteady and mysterious combination of weakness and strength: "When I am weak, then I am strong" (2 Cor. 12:10). In his letter to the Romans, written toward the end of his life, Paul even suggests developmental stages of Christian virtue: "Suffering produces endurance, and endurance produces character, and character produces hope. . . ." (5:3–4).

SIN AND MATURITY

For the Christian, maturity is always understood in terms of both grace and sin. How is sin involved in Christian development? Here again, the relationship is understood in various ways in the Christian tradition.

One powerful Christian metaphor of human perfection is that of childlikeness. In the context of preparedness for the Kingdom of God, Jesus encouraged his followers to "turn and become like children" (Matt. 18:3; see also Mark 10:14–15 and Luke 18:16–17). This ideal of innocence and sinlessness appears to argue for a "holy immaturity." Paul's use of different words to dis-

---

5. Calvin's remarks are from his *New Testament Commentaries*, 11:182–84. Our emphasis.

6. In some strands of Roman Catholic tradition this plateau is not occupied exclusively by Christ. The male clergy, who represent the manhood of Christ and stand in his place, may be called "father." The children of God, by subtle extrapolation, become the children of the hierarchy. Thus the unfortunate dichotomy of lay/clergy is deepened further in the child/parent metaphor.

tinguish children as immature (*nēpioi*) from children as offspring and heirs of God (*tekna*) clarifies this ideal of childhood.[7] Infants (*nēpioi*) are characteristically "tossed to and fro and carried about with every wind of doctrine, by the cunning of men, by their craftiness in deceitful wiles" (Eph. 4:14). Children as sons and heirs exhibit two relationships which are also the goals of human maturing: They *belong* in a thorough and enriching fashion, and they do not foolishly consider themselves self-sufficient. Christian adults are called to such childlikeness—to recognize that they belong to God and to God's community and that, alone, they are insufficient to their own salvation.

Although, as an ideal of maturity, childhood appears to be non-developmental or even antidevelopmental, the distinction in the New Testament of different kinds of childhood allows for a movement from childishness to childlikeness. We will return in later chapters to a discussion of the role of the childlike traits of belonging and of a proper dependency in the process of adult maturing.

While childlikeness suggests an absence of sin, another aspect of personal growth suggests a positive correlation between maturing and "sin."[8] Development into autonomy entails a separation from, and often a rejection of, others' codes of behavior. Such culturally unacceptable behavior is frequently interpreted by these others as "sin." Autonomy here is best understood as the ability to ground one's behavior in the rightness of one's own experience and convictions instead of simply following (like a child) external mandates, be these familial, cultural, or religious. Jesus' behavior in regard to the rules of the Sabbath (e.g., Matt. 12:1–13) is an illustration of such autonomy and "sinfulness."

Christian experience has long recognized another and more paradoxical relationship between sin and religious growth. It was sin

7. *Nēpioi* is found in Eph. 4:14, Gal. 4:1 and 3, 1 Cor. 3:1 and 13:11, and Rom. 2:20. For Paul's use of *tekna* see, for example, Eph. 5:1 and 6:1, 1 Thess. 2:7 and 11, and Rom. 9:8. In 1 Cor. 14:20 Paul uses the word *paidia* for "immature children." *Paidia* is used by the writers of the synoptic Gospels to signify that childhood or sonship necessary for entry into the Kingdom of God; see Mark 10:13–15, Matt. 18:2–5 and 19:13–14, and Luke 18:16–17.

8. A similar reflection on this relationship can be found in David Clines, "Sin and Maturity," *Journal of Psychology and Theology*, 5 (1977): 183–96.

that brought Christ into the world—in retrospect, a "happy fault" (*felix culpa*). Luther reminded believers that Christianity entails risk-taking and an energetic self-expression, which in turn involves the likelihood of error and sin. He determined to "sin bravely," aware both that his energetic activity would not work his salvation and that worse failure and stagnation awaited the person who did not dare.

While not directly concerned with the theological issue of sin, this book will examine crises, personal failure, and loss as these influence the process of adult development. We shall turn frequently to a consideration of these crucial experiences (sinful or not) and the reconciliation required as a person moves from one stage of life to the next.

RELIGIOUS DEVELOPMENT AND EDIFICATION

One of the most compelling images of human development in the New Testament is the architectural metaphor of "building up" (*oikodomein*, "edification"). At first glance this metaphor appears distant from the question of personal development and more germane to institutional growth. However the image of building up is personalized in the New Testament as the building up of the community as the body of Christ. This body-building metaphor is strong in Matthew and Luke. Matthew repeatedly returns to this image: the parable of building on a solid foundation or on sand (7:24–27); Christ's promise to build his Church on the rock of Peter (16:17–18); Jesus' reputed claim that if the temple of God were destroyed, he would build it up in three days (26:59–63, 27:39–40). Luke repeats the story of building on rock or on sand (6:46–49) and relates a parable of foolish construction —the man building new barns when that night he would die (12:16–21); in the context of discipleship Jesus insists on the need for planning before beginning to build, lest one be unable to complete the project (14:27–30).

The Pauline letters invoke this image repeatedly. The Thessalonians are called to "build one another up" (1 Thess. 5:11); the Romans are encouraged to "pursue what makes for peace and for mutual upbuilding" (14:19). This metaphor can be used in a nondevelopmental sense, as in the dualistic opposition of the otherworldly "building from God" and the "earthly tent" (2 Cor. 5:1). Most frequently, however, the Pauline writings describe the faithful themselves as this "building of God" under construction.[9] In the letter to the Ephesians, for example, the writer portrays the living body of the Church growing in co-ordination and maturity as it "upbuilds itself in love" (4:16).[10] A strength of this metaphor of development in the New Testament is its corporate aspect. The body being developed is not that of an individual; Christian growth is never simply an individual enterprise. The developing body is the communal corpus of believers in which Christ and the Spirit abide.

In the coming chapters we will describe adulthood and explore Christian maturity not as a settling down on a familiar plateau but as a journey over more interesting, if less charted, terrain. It is a journey on which the pilgrims may experience themselves as mature, as "well begun," but also as needing to press on. The ideal of Christian maturity will not be located at some specific point on the developmental spectrum (either in the innocence of childhood or in some final and completed perfection) but will be discovered at each stage of adult growth, in appropriate response to the challenges of that stage. The religious transformations to which we shall attend are not those of conversion in its most radical sense. We shall chronicle instead the religious development that accompanies the sometimes traumatic but more frequently gradual maturation that describes adult life. Thus we hope to illumine a contemporary pattern of Christian growth, a current schedule for Paul's injunction to "press on" toward the fullness of life.

9. In Paul's letter to the Ephesians another word, "grow" (*auxanein*, "augment"), is used to describe the development of the "household of God," of which "Jesus himself [is] the cornerstone" (2:19–21). In Eph. 4:15–16 and Col. 2:19 this word for growth is applied to the developing body of Christ, the communal body of believers.

In the synoptic Gospels this augmenting appears in agricultural metaphors: the lilies of the field (Matt. 6:28), the mustard seed (Matt. 13:31–32), and the parable of the sower and the seed (Mark 4:8). The Christian paradox of personal growth is suggested in John 3:30, where John the Baptist describes his relationship with Jesus: "He must increase, but I must decrease."

10. Bornkamm (1971, p. 242) alludes to this image of the cosmic body of the Church as one of the indications that Paul did not write this letter. Beyond the question of Paul's authorship, the passage presents a mixed metaphor of development: development from childhood into adulthood (vv. 13–14) is surrounded by a conflicting image of corporate growth—all the parts of the body growing together "into . . . the head" (vv. 12, 15–16).

CHRISTIAN VIRTUE, PSYCHOLOGICAL STRENGTH, PERSONAL SKILL

Growth in adult life means a growth in power. Such power, both attractive and frightening, can be understood as psychological strength, as Christian virtue, and as behavioral skill. The ambiguity of adult power recommends that we clarify these three perspectives and the relations that exist among them.

Erikson interprets adult growth as a gradual emergence, testing, and consolidation of personal resources over the course of adult life. These resources are described as "potentialities for significant interaction" (IYC, p. 93). They are psychosocial strengths; that is, capabilities of the person for consistent and competent action in the world. Erikson himself has reflected on the nexus between these psychosocial strengths and virtue. In exploring "the developmental roots . . . of certain basic human qualities which I will call virtues," his deepest interest is in the personal and societal continuity that such virtues ensure. For humankind's "psychological survival is safeguarded only by vital virtues which develop in the interplay of successive and overlapping generations" (IR, p. 114).

Erikson does not present a systematic treatment of the relationship between psychosocial strengths and virtues. He does, however, suggest that over the developmental course each psychological resource reaches its fullness as an enduring disposition, a persistent strength which can survive subsequent losses and difficulties.

In Erikson's developmental schema a maturing adult is confronted with three crucial tasks: to become able to love and commit oneself to particular persons; to be creative and responsible for what one has generated; to discover and construct the meaning and value of one's life. A person's response to these tasks, especially as they arise in developmental crises, determines his or her growth in virtue.

For Erikson the psychosocial strength of intimacy develops into the virtue of love. This virtue is "the mutuality of devotion" and the "basis of ethical concern" (IR, pp. 129–30); it represents the adult transformation of the love one has received in childhood into an effective and consistent care for others. The strength of generativity develops into the virtue of care, "the widening concern for what has been generated by love, necessity, and chance" (IR, p. 131). The challenge of integrity, the ultimate developmental task of affirming the meaning of life, develops the virtue of wisdom—"detached concern with life itself, in the face of death itself" (IR, p. 133). In this virtue the paradoxical combination of personal investment and responsible renunciation, tested in all the developmental crises of adult growth, reaches its peak.

Don Browning (1973), commenting on Erikson's understanding of psychological virtue, stresses the synthetic aspect of these virtues. Psychosocial strengths develop into virtues as they balance a person's inclinations of commitment and withdrawal, controlling and letting go, engagement and renunciation. An example of this synthesis, this balancing of opposing forces in adult virtue, can be seen in the adolescent's development of the virtue of fidelity. The capacity for fidelity arises in the resolution of the challenge of personal identity. The virtue of fidelity is grounded in an enduring and stable sense of who I am. It is this stability which allows me to sustain loyalties. Yet questions of identity can be resolved in an unbalanced manner. I can construct an inflexible sense of self. Such rigidity, an instance of overcommitment, will hinder my ability to admit the changes in self that are necessary in the next developmental stage, that of intimacy. The intimacy challenge invites me to risk and alter the sense of self just recently established. Thus for Erikson virtue is a necessarily flexible strength since it must remain open to continued development.

How are these psychological virtues related to Christian virtue? In the Judeo-Christian tradition virtue in its most basic sense refers to a faithfulness to God (Léon-Dufour, 1967). Whether expressed as obedience to the will of God or more lyrically as "walking with God" (Gen. 5:22–24, 6:9), virtue describes the response of the believer to God's presence in life. For the contemporary Christian, we suggest, this presence can be discerned within the structure and tasks of adult growth—not only in its patterned unfolding but in its crises and apparent disruptions of growth.

Adult development for a Christian is a growth that is grounded in specific motives, values, and convictions (exemplified in the Scriptures and in Christian history) and governed by definite images. Central among these images are those of a wandering, pilgrim people guided by their God, and the life-through-death example of Christ's death and resurrection. These governing images predict for believers the trajectory of their own development.

If the central virtues for the adult Christian are charity (*agapē*) and service (*diakonia*), Erikson's developmental schema can suggest specific ways that these virtues present themselves in adult life and the contemporary means by which they are developed or frustrated. Thus the call to Christian charity can be clarified by Erikson's reminder that the somewhat idealized "love for all persons" proper for an adolescent is no longer fitting for the young adult, who is now called to a commitment to particular individuals. Christian service or *diakonia* is better understood as one grasps the complex challenge in generativity of learning to care for others without controlling them.

Finally, aware that God's ways are not our ways and that the cross is a central dynamic of religious growth, the Christian is well prepared to discern God's active presence within the surprising and often painful crises and transitions of adult life. Likewise, a Christian recognizes growth in virtue as both a task of personal development (the responsibility, even the asceticism, of Christian adulthood) and a gift. Christians are those who are surprised and grateful to be graced with the strengths that allow them to love well and to care for what they and others have generated.

This nexus between psychological strength and Christian virtue also raises the question of skillful behavior. A virtuous person is a skillful person; skills are the ways in which virtues are expressed. A successful resolution of the developmental challenges of adult life releases personality resources which enable the adult to interact effectively within his or her society. The Christian can, in grace, be disposed toward justice and mercy. These dispositions are essential, but, of course, they are not enough. The psychological capacity and the religious motive must be strengthened and matured in one's actions. Attitudes must be translated into appropriate behavior.

Growth in Christian virtue is not only a function of inspiration, religious education, and good example. It is influenced as well by the ability to act skillfully. The Christian injunction to love one another, for example, is complemented by learning how to express and engender this love. Loving entails more than good feelings or proper attitudes; it involves certain behaviors—sharing of myself, empathy with others, confrontation (Egan and Cowan, 1979). To share myself with another, I must be psychologically disposed, able to overcome the hesitancy suggested by fear or suspicion or shame. But, these overcome, I must be able actually to share—to disclose myself in a way that is appropriate for me and for the situation. Appropriate self-disclosure can be complicated. But I am not, however, limited to my current level of success. I can become more skillful, learning better ways to express my needs, my ideas, my feelings, my objectives.

This is equally true in empathy. An essential psychological strength undergirds my ability to stand with another, emotionally and intellectually. This resource may be reinforced by my commitment to see Christ in the persons who come into my life. But these basic attitudes may not be enough. My capacity for accurate empathy can be enhanced by my development of a range of behavioral skills. An accepting posture, attentive listening, sensitive paraphrasing—each can contribute to my effective presence with another.

Confrontation, too, makes a critical contribution to effective love. Here "confrontation" is not limited to its negative and narrow connotation as interpersonal conflict. An ability to confront involves the psychological strength to give (and receive) emotionally significant information in a way that leads to self-examination rather than to self-defense. To do this, I need to be skillful in communicating nonjudgmentally and in dealing with anger in myself and in others.

Another example may illumine the connection between religious intent and skill training. At the heart of Christian spirituality is the discipline of self-knowledge. This Christian self-knowledge includes freedom from both blind passion and social pressures; it seeks an awareness of God's gracious presence in my life. It is a strength that can be expected to characterize the mature Christian. Yet the question often remains: How does the Christian become spiritually aware? Do I *will* such awareness? Do I pray for it? Do I submit to a spiritual master? Each of these approaches may be useful. Today these can be complemented by training in the skills of personal reflection. The use of the personal journal, prayerful access to one's imagination, exercises in value clarification—these tools of self-awareness are open to Christian purpose. And training in these skills can give added content to an important Christian ideal.

The word "skill" has an unpleasant ring to many today. It is true, to be sure, that if behavioral skills are not informed by a capacity for genuine concern, they remain hollow and ineffective. They may even be used manipulatively. It is equally true, however, that religious impulses can be frustrated and the challenges of maturity exaggerated by the lack of these basic skills of interaction. The negative reaction to skills and skills training is perhaps reinforced by the plethora of how-to-do-it books in recent years, many of these banal or exploitative. Yet skills, however learned, remain indispensable components of effective behavior and, further, the stuff of Christian asceticism. A danger inherent in skill training lies in its potential disengagement from a positive value system. Skills are neutral and can be used to manipulate and control as well as to love. They take on Christian purpose when located within the Christian value system. Christian values and images can ground these interpersonal skills and Christian motives shape their purposes.

Skill training is, of course, no panacea; it will neither transform the unmotivated nor substitute for a community's powerful witness of Christian living. Yet skillful behavior is an essential part of a mature and virtuous life. It is our conviction, to which we shall return in later chapters, that the emerging technology of skill training can be a valuable resource for religious growth in adulthood.

A FINAL CAUTION

As we move toward our consideration of the particular challenges of religious adulthood, let us pay particular attention to a caution that Erikson himself raises. Intimacy, generativity, and integrity are sometimes discussed as if each were an unambiguously positive achievement of maturity. The negative components that are equally important to personality development in each of these stages are omitted. If it is easy to slip into such thinking, it is also in error. Our understanding of development is not served by reducing these terms to only their positive connotations. The negative impulses that are released in each of the stages of adult development—impulses toward isolation, self-concern, resentment, and doubt—"are and remain the dynamic counterpart" (CS, p. 274) of those developmental impulses that are valued more posi-

tively by oneself and one's culture. Adult development neither results from nor produces conflict-free existence. As we saw earlier
in this chapter, both negative and positive impulses are evoked at
each stage. Each contributes its power to one's movement toward
maturity. Positive and negative factors emerge together and struggle against each other in the crisis that defines the developmental
challenge. The young adult experiences both the desire to merge
with others and the impulse to hold back in order to protect an
emerging sense of self. Neither "intimacy with all" nor "isolation
from all" describes maturity. The adult capacity to be with other
people in a variety of appropriate ways is developed in the struggle
to balance these opposing impulses of intimacy and isolation. And
these opposing impulses remain in the adult personality. It is not
the "goal" of each stage to eradicate those elements which are
seen as undesirable by a person's conscience or culture. Lasting
strengths of the adult personality result from the balance of both
positive and negative impulses in a ratio that is appropriate to the
individual and consistent with his or her life commitments. Erikson warns us against "stripping the stages of everything but
their 'achievements'" and dismissing the developmental significance of "the paradoxes and tragic potential of human life."
This denial will only impoverish us, as individuals and as a people,
and "make us inept in a heightened struggle for a meaningful existence" (CS, p. 274). Models of development that leave room for
an appreciation of the paradox and ambiguity of life are more useful than those limited to the forced clarity that dualism provides.

Finally, the resources that emerge at each stage of adult development are sometimes discussed as if these were desirable qualities that the determined "developer" should seek after with reso-
lute purpose. Such "achievement" language can be misleading, as
the subtleties of personal maturity disintegrate into a checklist of
prescribed adult experiences. More importantly, the nuances of
receptivity and readiness are lost. Maturity proceeds in its own
time. It is not often the reward of aggressive pursuit. Erikson sees
his own theory of development as "only a tool to think with" and
warns that it not be turned into "a prescription to abide by" (CS,
p. 270). We shall attempt to be mindful of this caution in the
chapters ahead as we offer Erikson's theory as a tool with which to
think about religious adulthood.

TWO

Adult Crisis: Psychological Structure and Religious Meaning

"Crisis" is a term we use often in this book. Take time here to locate the word in your own experience. What have been the critical times, the decisive or crucial events in your life? What are the turning points that chart your own history? Which of these have you experienced as "crises"? Spend some time in this recollection.

Choose one of these crises now for reflection. It may be the experience you recalled in the Reflection at the beginning of the first chapter, or some other that seems especially—perhaps even surprisingly—full for you. Let the experience become concrete again in your memory. Recall its onset, the circumstances, the people, the outcome. Take the time you need.

Then reflect on these questions:
How long were you "in crisis," engaged in this experience and its crucial issues?
What did you "lose" in this experience; what did you have to give up or set aside?
What did you "gain" in this critical transition; how were you enriched by this experience of crisis?

Adults grow and change in a wide variety of ways.[1] Some changes are substitutions: A different means is chosen to pursue the same goals and purposes in one's life. Such changes (for example, the move to a similar job in another firm) may be accomplished easily and without much disruption in an adult's life. A second category is that of simple, incremental change: A person develops a new level of skill or expertise but in a fashion that is continuous with former values and purposes. This growth, too, may entail little personal confusion or conflict. A third category of adult change—that of greatest interest in this book—is the often difficult and challenging growth involved in an adult crisis.[2]

The word "crisis" is so widely and variously used today that some delineation of its meaning here is important. We will most often use the term to signify the developmental challenges that can be expected to accompany a person's movement through adult life: challenges concerning how to be with others (intimacy), how to be creative and caring (generativity), and how to make sense of life (integrity). One's experience of these challenges is often triggered by a "marker event" (Levinson, 1978), a particular occurrence (marriage, divorce, job loss, promotion) that invites serious reflection and, possibly, reorientation. In our use of "crisis" we will retain the useful ambiguity between a crisis as a specific event and the broader life crises often induced by such occurrences.

It is useful to recall Erikson's distinction (IYC, p. 163) between a developmental crisis and a neurotic crisis. While ambiguity and disorientation may occur in both, a neurotic crisis is recognized by its dissipation of energy and its tendency toward isolation. A de-

---

1. In this chapter we are strongly influenced by the wisdom of our friend and colleague Rev. J. Gordon Myers, S.J. We are indebted to his contribution, from his work in crisis counseling and his lectures on adult growth, to our own developing understanding of the complexities of adult crisis.

2. Marris (1975) suggests parallel but slightly different categories of change: substitutional, growthful, loss. His third category, adult change due to loss, is discussed as a "crisis of discontinuity" (p. 24).

velopmental or "normative" crisis, on the other hand, is energizing and leads, however confusingly, to growth and further integration of the personality. Another characteristic of a developmental crisis is that it can be traversed; one grows through it rather than being overcome by it. Most often, however, in the midst of a crisis it is not clear whether it will lead to growth or to defeat. The recognition of a crisis as developmental or neurotic may be achieved only in hindsight. In this chapter we shall trace some of the responses by which an individual and a community can assist this ambiguous experience of crisis toward developmental resolution.

These developmental crises, "crucial period[s] of increased vulnerability and heightened potential" (IYC, p. 96), provide a fruitful focus for the study of both psychological and religious growth in adulthood. For only in a crisis, as Erikson notes, "does it become obvious what a sensitive combination of interrelated factors the human personality is—a combination of capacities created in the distant past and of opportunities divined in the present" (YML, p. 14). The crises of intimacy, generativity, and integrity, as we have noted, are often confronted in quite particular events: divorce, the death of a loved one, an important career change, retirement. The severity and disorientation of these adult transitions are experienced along a continuum. One person may experience retirement, for example, as an invigorating challenge, whereas for another it is a shattering disruption of the sense of self. In the following analysis we will explore the factors which contribute to a successful resolution of an adult crisis. We will examine first the structure of a crisis and then its internal dynamic.

THE STRUCTURE OF ADULT CRISIS

Three distinct phases can be noted in the experience of adult crisis—entry, duration, and resolution. The advent of, or entry into, a crisis may be either abrupt or gradual. A sudden personal loss (the death of a child, or loss of one's job) will usually signal a more traumatic entry into crisis, but a crisis that is brought on more gradually (a growing uneasiness with a failing marriage, or one's approaching retirement) may lead to an experience that is equally profound. The entry into crisis may be precipitated by an apparently simple event, such as a move to a new neighborhood or a different work site. Such a move may, quite unexpectedly, set off questions and doubts about one's abilities and relationships and values.

The unexpectedness of a developmental crisis is a key indicator of its likely severity. Many of the transitions of adult life (menopause, retirement, widowhood) are patterned and expected. The change may not be desired or preferred, but it is known to be inevitable or at least highly likely. Thus a married woman in middle age, aware that she will likely outlive her husband, may "rehearse" for widowhood (Neugarten, 1970). Other transitions are similarly anticipated—the medical student imagines herself as a doctor, the fifty-year-old worker rehearses for retirement. Thus expected, the transition through such a critical time may be invigorating rather than traumatic; the transition is foreseen, and one is somewhat prepared for the changes and adjustments it demands.

This expectation of an adult crisis points to the important role of "scheduling" in successful transitions. A critical transition that occurs "on schedule"[3] is more likely to be negotiated smoothly. The severity of a crisis is often related to its being unscheduled. The death of a child (rather than of one's aged parent), a sudden divorce (rather than widowhood in old age), an unanticipated job loss (rather than retirement)—these are events likely to introduce disruption into one's life and, thus, to lead to a "crisis" in the more popular sense of the word.

Other transitions may be *misscheduled*, either occurring prematurely or delayed. A premature transition may be the teen-age marriage in which a couple is faced with the challenges of interpersonal intimacy before resolving sufficiently issues of personal identity. A delayed crisis may be a couple's effort to resolve, after their children have grown and left home, aspects of their own intimacy relationship that were avoided in their first years of marriage.

Adult transitions may also be *overscheduled*. Certain patterns of adult life, such as marriage in one's early twenties, can become so expected that an adult may feel constrained to follow a schedule of development that does not fit personally. Thus a person

3. For a broader discussion of age norms and age stratification in relation to the scheduling of adult crises, see part 1 of Bernice L. Neugarten's *Middle Age and Aging* (1968), and Matilda White Riley et al., *A Sociology of Age Stratification* (1970).

marries in the twenties in response to familial or broader cultural pressure rather than to a personal sense of readiness, or a gay adult enters a heterosexual marriage out of social convention.

The experience of the mid-stage of a crisis can be likened to being carried in the trough of a wave. This image points both to the crisis's duration and to one's sense that it is undergone. The middle period of a crisis is a time of challenge and disorientation. One's normal perspective no longer holds. The customary reference points that usually serve so well now become less sure; they may even seem useless. An experience at the heart of a crisis is that of loss. The terror that may accompany a crisis arises in the question of whether the person will survive this loss.

The duration of a crisis is of considerable importance. A developmental crisis in adult life may extend over a period of several months or several years.[4] An adult transition which requires less time we generally do not understand as a crisis; a transition that endures beyond several years suggests that development has not occurred, that the person has been overcome by the crisis rather than having moved through it. Time is required to work through the experience of loss and to resolve the questions about oneself that are set off in the crisis. A community, a minister, a counselor contribute to the negotiation of a crisis by pacing a person through this time. Such pacing allows a person in crisis to confront the transition and to mourn the loss; this pacing also holds out the expectation of the gradual incorporation of this loss into a new, postcrisis understanding of oneself. Later we shall explore further this role of the community in pacing an individual through a crisis.

The successful resolution of a crisis is accomplished as a person completes the process of working through the change and loss of the transition. This may take the form of an assertive decision about the next phase of life or a more passive and mysterious realization that the work of mourning and personal reorganization

4. In his "Managing People Through Crises" (1971) Norris Hansell addresses the more delimited crises met in many organizational contexts. He reckons such crises as having a duration of twenty to forty days. Peter Marris (1975), analyzing the crises precipitated by the death of a spouse and by radical urban change, alludes several times to the duration of such crises as about two years (pp. 30, 48). Our own experience with adults in transition confirms these boundaries.

has been completed. The final stage of crisis is one of exit: The person "moves beyond" to a new stage of life and a new sense of self.

THE DYNAMIC OF ADULT CRISIS

A first characteristic of crisis is disorientation. Entering a critical transition, a person will likely begin to lose his bearings; the ordinary reference points that previously anchored his values and sense of self no longer avail. He may become uncharacteristically distracted as his attention becomes "migratory" (Hansell, 1971), as if scanning for a way to explain what is happening and to counteract the growing sense of loss of control. Disorientation arises from the experience of discontinuity and loss. The loss may be obvious, as in the death of a loved one, or it may be much less clear. The personal confusion of many critical transitions is heightened because one remains unable to name what is being lost. In the crisis precipitated by a troubled marriage or an unsatisfactory career, the person may search—sometimes in vain—for "what is wrong." This is an effort to identify what is being lost, what the person must give up in order to grow through the crisis. The marriage or the career itself may not be lost, but some aspect of it—once stable and even cherished but now unsatisfactory—may have to be let go. Marris (1975) and other students of change interpret this loss in terms of bereavement. The work of bereavement is to acknowledge and mourn the loss, while gradually letting go of the lost object. The task is thus dual: to identify and accept the loss while reinterpreting one's life so that the positive value of the lost object survives. The challenging nature of this dual task can be seen in the crisis of divorce or of a significant vocational change: The person must admit the loss, neither denying that it has happened nor rejecting altogether that part of life that is now past.

This process of working through a crisis is rarely described by a calm transition from stability through loss to stability. The inner dynamic of a critical transition often involves much ambivalence. In its more traumatic form (where the underlying dynamic is more starkly visible) a person in crisis suffers deeply from feelings of isolation, yet insists—even to close friends—"I just want to be left alone." This ambivalence may take the shape of alternating between denying the loss ("Nothing is the matter") and being overwhelmed by it ("Nothing matters any more"). An important learning for those who would understand the dynamic of crisis is that this ambivalence is not merely negative; it is not simply an unfortunate by-product of a person's pain but is an essential part of the reorientation and growth possible in a critical transition. To sustain a person in this pregnant ambiguity can contribute more to the ultimate resolution of the crisis than to force clarity and thus to foreclose options. Thus a ministry to adults in crisis will not seek to distract them from their very real confusion but will provide the support and challenge in which this ambivalence can be faced and worked through. A community of believers can learn to recognize and allow for such ambivalence among its members. Religious education can alert Christians to expect ambiguity in their adult lives—not only as a threat to be endured but as a positive contribution to their growth.

These disconcerting aspects of a crisis, then—its disorientation, ambivalence, loss—are not solely negative; the same factors create the opportunity for exceptional growth. The potential of such critical periods can be described from several perspectives. In her analysis of cultural transitions, anthropologist Mary Douglas speaks of "the potency of disorder" (1966, p. 94).[5] The chaos and disorder of a transitional state clear space for innovative ways of reordering the self. Psychiatrist Norris Hansell alludes to the "unusual flexibility" of adults in crisis and to their "peculiarly extensive capacity for change." When "the identity is not very clear, the capacity for learning is enlarged, and the individual is free to step into roles that he was too constrained to experience previously" (1971, p. 2). Sociologist Richard Sennett observes this potential for growth in a more Eriksonian perspective: "The essence of human development is that growth occurs when old routines break down, when old parts are no longer enough for the needs of the new organism" (1970, p. 98). The extraordinary, if unstable, openness to growth experienced by many in crisis can be used to advantage. Those who seek to minister to or assist adults in crisis can nurture growth in three specific ways: by structuring protective environments within which the confusing ambiguity can be probed rather than avoided, by forecasting a successful resolution

5. The context is her discussion of the role of ritual in guiding a person through transitional states; disorder and its potency are experienced in these margins between more ordered, stable periods of life.

of the crisis, and by supplying concrete methods of decision making and personal planning.[6]

This openness to growth recalls a related characteristic of an adult crisis, the experience of passivity. Erikson speaks of those "life crises which make . . . patients out of people" (YML, p. 14). "Patient" here has a larger than clinical meaning; it refers more broadly to the experience of "undergoing," or being "subjected" to a crisis. Adults rarely *choose* to enter the critical transitions of life; rather these crises "happen to" them. This passivity has its own threat. It suggests a loss of control, a vulnerability that may be inconsistent with one's learned expectations about being a grownup. Discussing Luther's development through crisis, Erikson observes the need for an adult to learn "that deep passivity which permits him to let the data of his competency speak to him" (YML, p. 207). The enforced passivity of adult crises can lead to an experience of receptivity which can complement the sense of dominance that characterizes adult experience and expectation.

To highlight such passivity is not to ignore the need for action and choice during a crisis; it is one's decisions and actions which will determine the successful transition. A simple surrender to the passive experience of a crisis suggests that one is overcome by it rather than that one has worked through it. As a characteristic of crisis, passivity points to the shift in the balance of receptivity and agency. During this time a person can learn to "experience" (Erikson's word for being passive) in a way that both modifies and enhances one's agency and control in the other areas of adult life.

The loss and passivity experienced in a critical transition signal the psychological strength especially tested and developed in a crisis—the ability to let go. In the midst of a crisis a person is often challenged to let go some part of self, even before it is clear what will replace this loss. Overcommitment to that aspect of self which seems threatened may lead to an inability to let go and to trust oneself to the next stage of life. Persons dare to let go only to the extent that they trust they will survive the loss.

Both the dynamic of an adult transition and its successful reso-

6. Hansell, (1970) in particular argues the appropriateness of teaching methods of decision making to persons in the midst of crisis. These skills provide concrete help and also assist the person in crisis to regain a sense of personal agency and control; they enhance "the dignity of individuals and the growth opportunity at crisis-in-transit" (p. 467).

lution are best understood against the backdrop of failure to negotiate crisis. Marris, reflecting on the relation of grief and crises
(1975, pp. 30 ff.), observes three ineffective modes of grieving. In
the first, grief is *delayed*; the person attempts to overlook the loss
by becoming busily occupied in a range of distracting activities.
This attempt is rarely successful. The delayed and pent-up grief
will often reappear as an exaggerated response to a subsequent
and seemingly minor disappointment.

The second ineffective response is to *inhibit* grief. Here the pain
of the loss is not confronted directly but is displaced into other
symptoms, perhaps headaches or fatigue. Both these responses are
attempts to deny the loss and to disguise the grief. If the experience of a crisis is to be growthful, however, the loss must be acknowledged and even mourned. Postponement of this mourning
will delay movement through the crisis. The denial of the loss will
close off the possibilities of growth and renewal that lie hidden
within the distress.

The third ineffective response is *chronic* grief. The person here is
overwhelmed by the loss and slips into static depression. A classic
instance of chronic grief is seen in the effort to keep the deceased
loved one's room "just as it was." There is an attempt to stop the
movement of time as the grieving person's energies go into defending against the full effect of the loss. Disoriented by the crisis,
the person cannot integrate the loss into an ongoing life but set-
tles into chronic mourning.

THE ROLE OF THE COMMUNITY

The disorientation experienced by a person in crisis extends also
to his or her social network or community. A person may feel
both lonely for and alienated from her usual friends; she may feel,
simultaneously, the need to be comforted and the need to be left
alone. This raises the question of the proper role of the community—loved ones and close associates—toward the person in the
midst of a critical adult transition.

One response of the community is to ignore. Those closest to
the person in crisis insist, "Everything is fine; don't worry about a
thing." It is often the community's own embarrassment and discomfort that motivate this response. The hope implicit here is
that, if the crisis and loss are ignored, they will go away. The com-

munity attempts to protect the individual (and, perhaps more importantly, itself) from the crisis, instead of helping the person to work through the demands of this difficult experience.

A second response of the community is to distract. The person in crisis is kept busy or, worse, is sent away on a vacation. Making a vacation possible may appear, at first glance, to be an act of kindness. Most often, however, it serves as an act of banishment. It removes the person from the environment in which the resolution must be achieved and from the network of friends who can provide support and challenge.

A third response is to blame. The person is reproached for being in crisis. Here attention focuses on the erratic behavior a person in crisis may display rather than on that behavior which is competent and more consistent with the person's enduring personality. The effect of this selective focus is to predict failure rather than the successful negotiation of the crisis.

A fourth response, more developmentally sound, is founded in the conviction that a crisis is best dealt with in one's usual environment. The response of the community here is to "foreclose on exit" (Hansell, 1971), to keep the individual within the supportive bounds of the community, selectively attending to the person's best hopes rather than his or her erratic behavior or pessimistic expectations. The community—perhaps assisted, but not replaced, by the professional helper—forecasts the successful resolution of the crisis. It supports the individual while it continues to expect competent behavior. The supportive community is not one that shies away from all conflict. The person in crisis must be confronted about actions that are harmful and behavior that is ineffective, but in a context of care and challenge rather than blame. Recognizing that it cannot itself resolve the crisis, the community is aware that it can assist and encourage the movement toward resolution.

This encouragement may take a variety of forms. Communities today are challenged to develop rites, religious or secular, which will allow persons to confront the losses of crisis (neither denying nor being morbidly overcome by them) and gradually to integrate these losses into a new yet continuous sense of self. As Gorer (1965) remarks concerning mourning customs around the crisis of death, such rites will be "time-limited" and have as one of their purposes the pacing of an individual through the stages of ac-

knowledging the loss, grieving, and gradually letting go that which
has been lost. In our discussion of the religious response to crisis
we shall consider the forms that these adult rites of passage may
take.

CRISIS AS A RELIGIOUS EVENT

What is the religious meaning of this paradoxical pattern of
growth in human life? Crises by their very structure invite an
adult to a re-examination and even a reorientation of her or his
life. The believer can recognize—in the patterns of human growth
and in the critical periods of disruption, loss, and gain—special opportunities for religious growth. In the disorientation of a crisis
the believer can experience the inbreaking of God, who challenges
conventional insights and plans; in the journey through and beyond the pain of a crisis the believer can experience the grace of
deliverance, the gift of being empowered to live a new and better
life with God.

A Christian reflection on crisis as a religious event may begin in
the New Testament interpretation of *krisis*. Three elements of the
New Testament meaning are relevant: *krisis* is judgment; it is
most often the judgment of God or of his son Jesus; it is a judgment to be delivered at the end of life.[7]

A clue to the understanding of this New Testament concept in
a developmental context can be found in its use in the letter to
the Hebrews (9:27). Here the author argues that Christ has appeared once and for all in human history to redeem humankind.
The argument is introduced with the phrase "just as it is ap-
pointed for men to die once, and after that comes judgment
[*krisis*]. . . ." A developmental notion of crisis suggests that we
die repeatedly as we negotiate the transitions of loss and gain that
constitute the major crises of our lives. In the midst of each crisis

7. See especially Matt. 10, 12, and 23 for *krisis* as God's judgment; this is a
final judgment in both Matt. 12:36 and John 5:24–29. While the tone of
krisis in the New Testament is most often judgment as condemnatory, the
strongest statement of this occurs in John 5:24, where it is stated that the
believer is *not* judged, does not come to *krisis*, but passes from death to life.
Here *krisis* (condemnation) is opposed to *zoē* (life). For a full analysis of
krisis in the fourth Gospel see Blank (1964). See also Bernd Jaspert (1976)
on crisis as a category in Christian church history.

we experience the demand for decision, for judgment (*krisis*). Yet accompanying this demand for agency and decision is the experience of a particular receptivity, related to the lessening of our control and self-confidence. Believers and nonbelievers alike report the resolution of a crisis as something that has *happened to* them. Religious faith recognizes in this passivity and receptivity of a crisis a special openness to the presence of God.

The developmental meaning of crisis resonates with the characteristics of the New Testament *krisis* in its assessment of this time of decision as an "end-time." Most often a crisis does not signal the end of one's life, but it does mark the end of one stage in life. When the attendant experiences of loss and grief are traumatic, this end-time event may share the eschatological and even apocalyptic awareness of the *krisis* of the New Testament. The belief that such a critical experience signals the inbreaking of God in my life, or that the decision to be made in an adult crisis has to do with God's plan for my future, is not an element in a psychological theory of development. Such an interpretation derives from the Christian vision; it is this vision that renders human development religious.

The New Testament also portrays for us the adult crises of Jesus and Paul. Paul's experience of conversion[8] bears all the markings of a mid-career crisis. The Jewish activist Saul, in the midst of a zealous religious career,[9] suffers a breakdown. He experiences disorientation and confusion: Blinded, he remains so for several days; the voice he hears, others do not hear. Among the Christian community at Damascus, he is healed. His eyesight is restored, but now he sees differently, with a vision that leads to a radically different career. He has a new sense of self, even a new name. This story of Paul's conversion is a heightened example of

8. Paul makes a very terse reference to this event in his letter to the Galatians (1:13–17). The account in the Acts of the Apostles (9:1–22; parallel accounts in 22:4–16 and 26:9–18), written several decades later, relates a much fuller and more exciting story. If this account represents an embellishing of detail, it also enjoys the authority of its inclusion in Sacred Scripture.

9. Bornkamm (1971) reminds us that Paul's conversion was not from a life of unfaith: "When Paul was converted, it was not the case of a man without faith finding the way to God, but of one zealous for God, more in earnest than anyone else about his demands and promises" (p. 23).

an adult crisis,[10] dramatically illustrating its characteristics. There is the breakdown of the person's usual patterns, followed by a period of disorientation and isolation, then a movement—with the help of others—toward resolution. The sense of being led through the crisis and of being healed by God is, of course, what interprets the crisis *as religious*.

The Christian gospel is the good news about the crisis of Jesus Christ—his passion, death, and resurrection. The story told in the gospel argues that faith can find meaning in loss and death; Jesus Christ stands as the sign and guarantor that this is the pattern of life in which religious faith is tested and thrives. The account of Jesus in the garden of olives illustrates his experience of crisis.[11] This episode must appear scandalous to those who have learned to see Jesus, from his first moments of human life, as perfected—involved in neither growth nor its necessary companion, doubt. In the gospel account Jesus exhibits great disorientation; his former clear-sighted conviction about the direction of his life seems to have fallen into doubt. He becomes "sorrowful and troubled" (Matt. 26:37) and breaks into a severe sweat (Luke 22:44). He prays for a change of plans, that his Father might "let this cup pass" (Matt. 26:39). His distress and confusion show again in his irritation with his sleeping disciples. And in the midst of the anguish of this crisis he tries to trust in something that he no longer understands. But then—surprisingly, incongruously—Jesus finds himself strengthened, able to survive the crisis, to accept its demands and move courageously toward its resolution. He is at the same time strengthened in himself and empowered by his Father's will.

These two Christian stories exhibit an attractive complementarity: Out of Paul's confusion and disorientation comes a radically altered career;[12] from Jesus' distress comes a new resolve

10. Exegetes such as Bornkamm (1971), who are scandalized by the "unbalanced" behavior and its implied immaturity in such an important "grownup," struggle to downplay this account in the Acts of the Apostles of Paul's crisis. Bornkamm's portrait of Paul's change of heart is decidedly cool and rationalistic: "As a result of arguments with the hellenistic Christians in Damascus and elsewhere . . . it suddenly dawned on him who this Jesus really was" (p. 23).

11. See Matt. 26:36–46; Mark 14:32–42; Luke 22:39–46.

12. If the word "career" sounds offensively secular and inappropriate here, it is useful to recall its roots in the Sanskrit word *carya*, which indicates a path

in an earlier, but now more deeply understood, commitment. The ambiguity of a crisis is that in its midst it is uncertain whether and how a person will survive. What is the way out? What must be let go? The resolution of these questions cannot be found in any formula, however religious, but only gradually emerges from within the individual. With the help of loved ones, a believer slowly comes to understand where God is leading through this crisis.

An adult crisis becomes a religious event when the person recognizes in the experience the challenging and supportive presence of God. Such a recognition locates the disorder and threatened loss within a larger pattern,[13] rescuing it from absurdity and idiosyncrasy. A humanist in crisis may cling to the hope of an ultimately benevolent process working in life; a Christian in crisis is invited to identify his or her own experience of loss and gain with the life of Jesus Christ and the gospel paradox, "Unless a grain of wheat falls into the earth and dies, it remains alone; but if it dies, it bears much fruit" (John 12:24). To be able to identify one's own life with these revealed patterns of growth is recognized by a Christian as a gift. It is grace which enables me to see my own life —which sometimes appears so singular and even absurd—as sharing the patterns and purpose of the life of Jesus Christ.

A believer may also apprehend (although often only in hindsight) the specifically religious dynamic of an adult crisis: being emptied[14] of the control and self-determination that are usual in adult life, a person is given the space in which to envision new plans and possibilities. The "potency of disorder" in a crisis alters consciousness, permitting the person to perceive differently. It is precisely such altered consciousness that in turn allows the person

---

or trajectory that one's life follows in response to divine imperatives and urgings.

13. Theologians today speak of this pattern as the myth of Christianity. Here "myth" does not mean a fable but the *mythos* or plot and meaning of life. When life has no plot, no direction or sense, it becomes absurd and unbelievable.

14. The spirituality of crises is grounded in this dynamic of emptying: "Christ Jesus, . . . though he was in the form of God, did not count equality with God a thing to be grasped, but emptied himself, taking the form of a servant, being born in the likeness of men" (Phil. 2). Self-emptying, letting go one's previous way of living, is required for growth through crisis.

to perceive the usually imperceptible—the presence and activity of God.

The religious learning in a crisis is, as in most learning, by way of repetition. The person recalls that the losses and confusions of puberty and leaving adolescence led to a fuller life, and that the risk of identity in a love relationship led to a new and richer sense of self. So the pattern teaches that by letting go, I receive; by losing my life, I gain it. This learning—fragile, never completed, and always part faith—is preserved and transmitted in the Christian tradition. As I learn, in the repeated challenges of growth, the paradoxical lessons of crises, this learning becomes a resource both for my own later development and for the faith of the next generation.

ADULT CRISIS AS A RELIGIOUS PASSAGE

The structure and dynamic of an adult crisis point to a parallel image of human change, that of passage. A person "goes through" a crisis, as through a passage; both images suggest a kind of change that occurs by means of an ambiguous transition through danger. We will examine the inner structure of a passage and then turn to an exploration of a passage's explicitly religious and Christian character.

A Dutch anthropologist, Arnold van Gennep, working at the turn of this century, described the critical transitions of life in his *Les Rites de Passage* (see van Gennep, 1960). The classic passages in van Gennep's analysis were the incorporation into community at birth, the transition from childhood to adulthood, marriage, and death. The rites of passage were a community's response to the danger of these crucial transitions. With ritual a community symbolizes the danger and the loss involved in a passage; by so doing it protects the individual, tames the terror of the change, and facilitates the person's successful negotiation of the transition.

The heuristic study of passages by the contemporary anthropologist Victor Turner (1969 and 1972) focuses on their disruptive effect in the ordinary course of life. These passages are discussed as intervals of "liminality,"[15] *limen* being the boundary

15. For Turner, "liminality" names those intervals or passages between the ordinary experiences of social living. "Some of these intervals are 'sacred' and

or threshold that the person passes through. Following van Gennep, Turner distinguishes three stages in a passage: separation, transition, and incorporation.[16]

Separation occurs when a person is taken out of the ordinary flow of life; such a change necessarily entails loss and disorientation. "In liminal sacredness many of the relationships, values, norms, etc. which prevail in the domain of pragmatic structure are reversed, expunged, suspended, reinterpreted or replaced by a wholly other set" (Turner, 1972, p. 391). Separated, either abruptly or gradually, from the ordinary course of life, a person enters the middle phase of a passage. This phrase, which van Gennep called the stage of marginality, Turner more aptly, if arcanely, labels *cunicular*, "being in a tunnel." "Cunicular" recalls both the duration of this period and its characteristic darkness. Another image which catches the in-between experience of this time is that of a "no-man's land." During this time one is in a marginal and nameless state, neither what one was nor what one will be. The classic example of this is the adolescent caught between childhood and adulthood, exhibiting behavior proper to both states and confusing both himself and others. But adult experiences of transition—being legally divorced but not having psychologically "worked through" this passage, or contemplating a career change while still uncertain of one's future career—elicit the same kinds of ambiguity and confusion.

Although this middle phase of a passage is initially experienced as confusing and painful, Turner stresses the role of ritual in making this a positive experience. Ritual protects this period as a "free space," a time apart when the individual is allowed to perceive the ordinarily imperceptible, the deeper values obscured in the bustle of everyday life.[17] The most characteristic activity of this time is "the analysis of culture into factors and their free recombination in any and every possible pattern, however weird . . ." (1972, p.

may be termed 'anti-structural' in the social sense, for they represent a stripping and leveling of men before the transcendent" (1972, pp. 390–91).

16. Van Gennep's terms here are *séparation*, *marge*, and *agrégation*.

17. Turner (1972, p. 401) notes the meaning of "sacred" as "set apart"; this enforced being set apart (by a crisis, or passage, in one's life) allows one to get in touch with the deeper, nonprofane values in one's own life and in one's community.

482).[18] Turner here points to the central dynamic of a passage or crisis, described by Mary Douglas, as we noted earlier, as "the potency of disorder." The disorder at the heart of a passage, especially if attended by ritual, can result in a creative reordering of one's life and values. Another characteristic feature of a passage, as of a crisis, is the experience of passivity ("something is *happening to* me"). Turner alludes to this "patient" aspect of a passage by speaking of the person in transit as a passenger.

The third stage of a passage, that of incorporation, parallels the resolution of a crisis. A successful passage is completed when the person has let go a former state and grown into a new state. This new state in life is celebrated in the rite of passage which welcomes one to a new position in the community (for example, as an adult or as married).

If this is the essential structure of a passage, we have next to explore these passages as explicitly a part of Christian experience. The place to begin is with the archetypical passage in Judeo-Christian history.

THE EXODUS: PARADIGMATIC PASSAGE

The originating[19] passage for Jews and Christians is the exodus of Moses and his followers out of slavery in Egypt, through the desert, into a new life. This passage was social in character rather than simply personal, yet it manifests the characteristics of a religious crisis and transition.

Intolerable conditions in Egypt led Moses and his followers to flee that country in the direction of the desert. The entry into this passage was through the double danger of darkness and water, both of which were turned to Moses' advantage by Yahweh (Ex. 14:20–29). Yet even as the Hebrews began this first step into the passage, a central characteristic of such crises appeared: Some began to doubt—are we rushing into the desert only to die? Is it not better to live as slaves (Ex. 14:11–12)?

The Hebrews' long sojourn in the desert, understood tradi-

18. By "culture" here Turner means the ordinary structure of one's life. It is this which breaks down in a passage or crisis and demands reconstruction.

19. This passage is originating in that Israel, as the people of Yahweh, *came to be* during this passage. The rigors of another geographic passage helped to create and define a contemporary belief system: See Sumiya (1969).

tionally as of forty years' duration,[20] was the middle phase of the passage. During this period the Hebrews wandered geographically, while their minds vacillated, unsure of the wisdom of their departure from the security of slavery in Egypt.[21] Throughout this period of doubt and ambivalence, however, their belief survived that they were being led; the experience of passivity in the heart of a crisis or passage was expressed by the Hebrews as a persistent belief that they were (in Turner's vocabulary) "passengers" to a new land.

We have observed the irony of a crisis or passage: It is the very confusion and disorientation of the event that create space for new learnings and re-visioning. For the Hebrews this occurred at Mount Sinai (Ex. 19:1 to Num. 10:11), where they learned the new style of life that would mark them as Yahweh's people. The code and covenant received at Sinai were not merely part of a mid-crisis reorientation; they were part of the *invention* of a people. It was during this time that the once motley group began to understand its new identity as the people of Yahweh (Judg. 5:11 and 13).

Yet at the very time Moses was receiving these laws on Mount Sinai, his people were growing uncertain; under Aaron's leadership they went so far as to construct the image of another god (Ex. 32). Thus the entire sojourn in the desert was a time of vacillation, doubt, and failure.

The first move to resolve this prolonged passage, an attempted entry into Canaan from the south, ended in defeat. A long and slow journey followed which eventually led this group of believers into that land which eventually would be called Israel. Several features of this resolution stand out. None of the adults who originally fled Egypt (except two men) saw the resolution of this passage (Num. 14:26–35, 26:63–65). The loss was very real; they failed to complete the passage though it was their faith that allowed their children to realize its resolution. Secondly, it was a

20. This period of years means, more generally, a long time, a generation, or "a full complement of time" (see Anderson, 1975, p. 101). The meaning "a generation" is particularly apt, since it recalls that of those who entered the passage none survived to its resolution.

21. In Ex. 16:2–3 we read of the murmuring after "the fleshpots of Egypt." For other instances of this continual murmuring, see Anderson (1975), p. 78.

passage into identity; several bands of Hebrews entered the desert and the Israelites emerged. Through a period of social crisis, a group experienced itself as led by Yahweh and formed as a people. Much was lost in the desert (death and infidelities), and something new, the next stage of Israel's life, was begun.

If the exodus was a passage which forged the identity of a people, it can also be interpreted as an intimacy crisis. These years in the desert describe a protracted courtship between Yahweh and Israel, with covenants, infidelities, and reconciliations. This critical passage also exhibits a characteristic of mature generativity: These people gave themselves to something that they would not fully enjoy; knowing the promised land only in promise, their efforts made it a legacy for the next generation.

CRISIS, PASSAGE, AND THE EXPERIENCE OF TIME

The crises and passages that describe human growth not only occur over time, but often entail a change in the experience of time. Erikson (IYC, p. 169) has pointed to the time distortion experienced by many adolescents: A great urgency about time alternates with a loss of interest in time. Recent research in developmental psychology (Bortner and Hultsch, 1972; Levinson, 1978) has made us familiar with the shift in time perspective experienced in the mid-life transition: I begin to measure my life not in terms of time-since-birth, but as time-left-to-live. In his analysis of the structure of passages, Turner alludes to a distortion of usual time flow: A passage is "almost always thought of or portrayed by actors as a timeless condition, an eternal now, as 'a moment in and out of time,' or as a state to which the structural view of time is not applicable" (1972, p. 399). Marris's study of adult crises of loss (1975) indicated the need for a moratorium, a period of "free time" in which a person could work through the grief of the crisis. Vaillant describes the shift in the use of time within a crisis as the self's effort to "obtain a time-out to master changes in self-image" (1977, p. 10).

These all point to the intimate relationship between a crisis or passage and a person's experience of time. The lead that we will explore is that these special times and altered relationships with time are related to religious convictions about sacred time.

Different religious traditions,[22] including Christianity, have been aware of the qualitatively different experiences of time that have to do with revelation and the presence of the divine in human history. The vocabulary in ancient Greek that expressed this distinction was *chronos,* signifying secular, profane, ordinary, chronological time, and *kairos,* sacred time and the time of the special presence of the Holy.

Israel resisted the identification, made in other religions, of sacred time with the regular and determined cycle of nature, but did follow their recognition of time as possessing a holy pattern.[23] For the Israelites this recognition was expressed in the Sabbath as a scheduled holy time and in the celebration of seasonal feasts to commemorate the historical actions of Yahweh. A dominant interpretation of sacred time in the Old Testament focuses on Yahweh's breaking into history; this happens at different key moments in history and will occur most decisively at the end of time, in "the day of Yahweh" (Amos 5:18; Is. 2:12).

In the New Testament this sense of sacred time receives a new urgency in the realization that Jesus' presence has ushered in a different kind of time, a special time of salvation. *Kairos* is used to note the beginning of Jesus' career: "The time [*kairos*] is fulfilled, and the kingdom of God is at hand" (Mark 1:15). This word more pointedly refers to Jesus' entry into the crisis of his passion. With the arrival of the fateful Passover he senses, "My time [*kairos*] is at hand" (Matt. 26:18).

While *kairos* is used often in the New Testament to signify the time of the special saving presence of God, *chronos* is not used systematically to mean secular or profane time.[24] There are, how-

22. See the typically sweeping presentation of sacred time in Eliade (1958), especially chap. 11.

23. The prophet Hosea (2:11) warned Israel against the worship of other gods in seasonal feasts. For a brief account of views of sacred time in the Old and New Testaments, see Léon-Dufour (1967), pp. 600–6.

24. There is no consistency in the New Testament usage of these two terms. *Chronos,* for example, is used in reference to times of particular religious relevance in Matt. 2:7 (the time of the coming of the star of Bethlehem) and Luke 1:57 (the time of Elizabeth's delivery of John). At several places (Acts 1:7 and 1 Thess. 5:1) *chronos* and *kairos* are used conjunctively to mean "the times and the seasons." See James Barr's critique (1962) of Marsh and J. A. T. Robinson for suggesting a simple and consistent distinction between these two words in the New Testament.

ever, at least four passages in the New Testament that employ *chronos* in a fashion that gives the connotation of ordinary, non-salvific duration.

In the Gospel of Mark Jesus responds to the possessed youth brought to him by asking, "How long a time [*chronos*] has he had this?" (9:21). In Luke's Gospel a similarly possessed man is portrayed as living inhumanly (in the wilds and without clothes) "for a long time [*chronos*]" (8:27). In the Gospel of John another person, ill for many years, is recognized by Jesus as having lain by a certain pool in Jerusalem "for a long time [*chronos*]" (5:6). In all three instances, *chronos* describes a prolonged duration of sickness. The healing of each of these persons concludes a long period of being chronically ill. The conclusion of Paul's letter to the Romans celebrates the present as a time of revelation of the mystery "kept secret for long ages [*chronos*]" (16:25). The word again translates the condition of history as chronic, awaiting the special time of the healing advent of the Christ.[25]

These chronic episodes, personal and cosmic, climax in the coming of God in Jesus. *Kairos*, in fact, refers to three different climaxes or end-times in the New Testament: the final and absolute end-time, brought on by God's judgment (*krisis*); the final period of history introduced by Jesus' coming; and specific points in history (individual or social) where one stage of life ends and another begins. John L. McKenzie describes this third meaning of *kairos* in the New Testament: "Each step in the process of time is a *kairos* in the sense that it is a critical time, a decisive moment which hastens or retards the *kairos* of salvation and judgment" (1965, p. 892). Some moments in personal and social time stand out in special significance. Ordinary duration is broken by the experience of *kairos*, which is, in Tillich's words, "qualitatively fulfilled time, the moment that is creation and fate. We call this fulfilled moment, the moment of time approaching us as fate and decision, *kairos*" (1936, p. 129).

It is the peculiar features of *kairos* as end-time and as saving presence of God that interest us in the context of adult crisis. Crises and passages have been seen to be end-times; the terror of

25. As Barr (1962) reminds us, chronology can be sacred, especially in the Old Testament. As such, it is personal and social history with an explicitly religious purpose and direction. Chronology as profane refers to history as unaware of the presence of God.

such transitions is precisely that something is being lost, some part or understanding of the person is coming to an end. Crises are potentially kairotic moments in their vulnerability, their peculiar openness to learning and to the re-visioning of life. For one who believes, a crisis is a place in which one might expect to encounter God. The anticipation of God's illuminating presence in such crises is reinforced by an exploration of similar times in one's past and God's guiding presence (at the time probably undiscerned) in these passages.[26]

A reflection on how we live in and use time can be aided by a review of *chronos* and *kairos* in our personal past. In such an exercise *chronos* would apply to those periods when life has moved along smoothly or at least busily. This can be called secular time, not because it is evil but because it is an ordinary and regular experience of time. Such periods can be filled with productivity or with boredom; what marks them as *chronos* are the characteristics of regularity and control. *Kairos*, then, may refer to transitions in one's life, when the regular flow of time is broken and (often, at least) a sense of control is threatened. The experience is of something (or someone) breaking into one's life. At first experienced as disorientation or loss, such a crisis or special time may, in retrospect, be recognized as a period of extraordinary growth. Often, it is *only* in such a recollection that we can realize the mysterious presence of God. Such a religious "recovery" of the past teaches us about the uneven and unexpected sacredness of our adult lives.

Two perils may accompany the effort to understand the sacred and profane times of our own life. Theologians have sometimes argued that *chronos* and *kairos* wrongly dichotomize time into secular and holy when in fact every moment is sacred and holds out the potential of encounter with God. This is true; but such a view easily ignores the unevenness of our experience of growth. Adulthood is not a plateau, psychologically or religiously. Adult growth is related to critical challenges and particular periods in life; it is the heightened consciousness and danger of such periods that suggest

26. Thus the need for practical exercises to allow an adult to grow in awareness of his or her past. Hidden within the dense experiences that constitute adult life are many special times—often times of crisis and pain—from which one can chart the course of one's own psychological and religious maturation. Without such experiential grounding, most adult religious education must remain largely theoretical and abstract.

their special gracefulness or holiness. A second peril concerns the routinization of *kairos*. This has various modes of expression, all destructive of holiness and psychological maturity. One mode is to stress the holiness of certain times to the eventual exclusion of others. This occurs both in the emphasizing of the holiness of a particular day (Sunday) to the neglect of the "daily holiness" of other times and in the stressing of the presence of God in Christian history to the exclusion of the divine presence in other religious traditions. Both represent efforts to locate the Holy definitively in time and, thus, to control it. This regularizing and controlling of sacred time eventuates in a safe but stale experience of God; *kairos* begins to look like *chronos*. The price of such control is often blindness to God's breaking into our lives in the unplanned and messy crises and passages that chart our psychological and religious growth.

THREE

Intimacy and Mutuality: The Challenge of Young Adulthood

Adulthood brings us together with other people in many different ways. In the next two chapters we will look at some of these. Let us begin this consideration in a personal reflection. First, spend some time with the vocabulary of relationships. As you read each word below, allow yourself to respond with those words, feelings, memories that make the word real for you. Take the time you need with each.

> *friendship*
> *teamwork*
> *love*
> *isolation*
> *sexuality*
> *co-operation*
> *competition*
> *loneliness*
> *mutuality*
> *devotion*
> *solitude*

Return now to one of the words, one which was particularly evocative, which recalled a full range of memories and feelings for you. Select one of these memories and allow it to become full again in your imagination. Recall the events, the persons, the circumstances, the feelings, the outcome that were part of it. Take some time with this.

Now ask yourself the following questions. There are, of course, no "right" or "wrong" answers here. The purpose is rather to give another chance for you to savor your personal experience of the joys and perils of adult relationships.

What does this experience say about your strengths for being with other people?

What does it suggest are the weaknesses or frustrations of your interpersonal style?

Are there clues here concerning ways in which your ability to be with others might be enhanced?

SEXUALITY AND INTIMACY

"Intimacy" often appears as a synonym for sexual expression or romantic sharing. We use this word in a broader psychological sense to refer to those strengths which enable a person to share deeply with another. These strengths come into play across a range of relationships—friendship, work collaboration, community living. Whenever there is personal disclosure and mutuality, intimacy is involved. A well-developed ability to be intimate enables me to be with different persons in a rich variety of different ways, ways that are appropriate to my own personality and to the demands of different situations. It is upon these intimacy resources that I draw in my attempts to live closely with others, to share my talents and ambitions, to merge my life and hopes with those of some one, some few others.

To help situate intimacy in a broadened context, one that goes beyond sexuality and romance, let us consider a crisis of intimacy that may arise in the course of one's work. I volunteer as a member of a work group where co-ordination and co-operation are necessary for the successful completion of our task. This may be a group at work, at school, in my church, or in the neighborhood. In the midst of this work I begin to feel uncomfortable. It is not that any one person is dominating the group or impeding its work. But my suggestion is only one among many. My work is affected by what the others do. My contributions look different to me after the group has dealt with them. I feel that things are not going as they should, as I expected they would. There is an impulse to gain greater control of the situation, countered by an impulse to withdraw. I vacillate in an experience of increasing discomfort and disorientation. But what is being threatened here? What is being lost? It is my very self. These others may overwhelm me, absorbing my identity as well as my ideas.

There are parallels here with the ambiguous experience of drawing close to another person in the more usual sense of intimacy. There are obvious differences, but the dynamic is the same. There is the threat of some loss of self. The temptation to flee is mixed with a desire to control the situation. Both these impulses are accompanied by an inclination to stay with the uneasiness, in the hope of finding a better way of being together and working together.

This example uncovers the underlying question of intimacy. Am I sure enough of myself and confident enough of my ability that I can risk being influenced through closeness with someone else? This is the psychological challenge of the early adult years. "The strength of any one stage is tested by the necessity to transcend it in such a way that the individual can take chances in the next stage with what is most vulnerably precious in the previous one" (CS, p. 263). Erikson begins his discussion of young adulthood here. The movement from adolescence into young adulthood involves a willingness to risk one's identity, that "vulnerably precious" sense of self that has emerged, not without struggle, over the teen-age years. As a young adult I must be able to come close to another person in a way that enables that person to know, to influence, and possibly to alter the boundaries of myself as I know them. I must accept the risk of being changed, of coming to a different awareness of who I am, as a result of such encounter. If I am unsure of who I am, if my movement through adolescence has left me still confused or deeply defended, then the risk implied in intimacy will seem too great. I will avoid closeness with others, either by refusing to enter any relationship that threatens to raise the possibility of intimacy or by developing such a rigid interpersonal style that there is no risk of my defended identity being questioned or attacked.

Intimacy involves an overlapping of space, a willingness to be influenced, an openness to the possibility of change. Only a strong and flexible identity can move toward intimacy. A diffuse identity is not defined enough to remain intact in the intimacy encounter. Mutuality is impossible. If I come close to you, I will be overwhelmed. A too rigidly defined identity makes mutuality equally impossible. There is too little flexibility in my sense of who I am, too little openness to learning something new about myself. Such a rigid sense of self is achieved through processes that psychologists describe as "identity foreclosure," a premature decision about personal identity that permits the adolescent to look away from the contradictions and ambiguities that haunt her or his awareness of self. Neither diffuse nor defended identity leaves much room for self-exploration. Close contacts with other people will seem a threat since they may force upon an individual information that can undermine the fragile sense of self. Or relations will be difficult to develop because a stereotyped interpersonal style keeps others at a distance and leaves no room for mutuality.

The move toward intimacy calls for a risk of the sense of self achieved through the resolution of the identity crisis. As Erikson notes, "True 'engagement' with others is the result and the test of firm self-delineation" (IYC, p. 124). The test is too severe for some adolescents, and their psychological development stumbles on this challenge. But more typical is the young person Erikson describes who, "emerging from the search for and the insistence on identity, is eager and willing to fuse his identity with that of others" (CS, p. 263). The dynamic of this internal development thrusts the individual into situations which provoke the release of new resources of personality.

We can see clearly here the elements of the intimacy challenge. Young adults are drawn, by internal awareness and social demands, toward experiences that call for self-disclosure, aware that these experiences may challenge much of what they believe about themselves. In moving toward closeness with people in the face of the risks involved, the young adult releases the psychological resources necessary for intimate living. These resources include both positive and negative impulses. One feels drawn toward self-disclosure and empathy, yet held back by caution or selectivity. Each of these is necessary for mature intimacy. And this maturity is approached as the young adult struggles to fashion a consistent interpersonal style, one which transforms the apparently contradictory impulses of intimacy and isolation into an appropriate personal expression.

SOCIAL CONTEXTS OF INTIMACY

There are many situations that call young adults to risk some part of their self-definition. It is in these contexts that one's resources for intimate living are evoked and strengthened. Among the most important of these, Erikson lists close friendship, group solidarity, sexual love and orgasm, social experiences of co-operation and competition, combative relationships, inspiring encounters with others and the experience of intuition from within oneself (CS, p. 264; ILC, p. 124). There is intriguing range and diversity here. It is not just sexuality that evokes intimacy. Sexual experience is a dramatic instance of the ambiguous power of mutual encounter. Romantic love is one of the most significant contexts in which the intimacy question is raised and is moved toward resolution for the young adult. But sexual intimacy is only part of psychological intimacy, even in marriage. An ability to perform sexually often precedes a capacity for emotional intimacy. In the mores of many contemporary relationships sexual sharing is an earlier stage, and easier to achieve, than psychological mutuality. These comments are not meant to dismiss or to depreciate the role of full genital mutuality in developing a capacity for psychological intimacy or in enriching intimate relationships. It is simply to note that intimacy and sexuality are not synonymous.

Intimacy is not just a factor in the socially "positive" relationships of friendship, co-operation, and love. In the combative relationships of argument and competition one has equal opportunity to test the limits of self and other and to experience the strain and exhilaration of mutual influence.

And intimacy is not just communal. Most experiences of intimacy do involve other persons. But an intuition from within can challenge profoundly the boundaries I set for myself, providing new information which calls into question my sense of who I am. I can learn to defend against such new information about myself, whether positive or negative. Or I can become more intimate with myself, open to the many voices of my interior world.

FRIENDSHIP AND SOLIDARITY

Friendship is a central instance of such intimacy relationship. One's experience with a close friend can provide personal examples of the kinds of sharing and challenge of which Erikson speaks. My friend is a person with whom I can share myself and who is open with me in return. My friend knows me well. This knowledge is a basis for much of the comfort and support my friend can offer me. This knowledge also makes my friend my most knowledgeable critic, a critic whose judgment I find it difficult to cast aside. It is because my friend knows me so well that I cannot easily dismiss the new information—both positive and problematic—that I receive in this friendship. Thus in friendship I can reveal myself, share my sense of my own identity. The friendship also tests that identity, challenges it with new information and modifies it through interaction with another autonomous self. One can look to one's own experience with a close friend to find examples of the overlapping of identities, the merging of selves, the intersection of lives that characterize intimacy experiences. Over time my relationship with a close friend provides a variety of situations which draw out and strengthen my ability to be with another person. My friendship thus both draws upon and further develops my capacities for intimacy.

Intimacy is similarly a part of many broader experiences of fellowship and group solidarity. There is a sense of cohesion that develops among comrades when important events have been experienced in common, even when there have not been personal expressions of emotional closeness. Such solidarity often characterizes military groups, novitiate and seminary classes, even some extended families. There is a bond of unity that can last, even when members separate or the group disbands. The ties are not those of personal sharing or direct disclosure but rather of a shared experience. These experiences of solidarity can also evoke one's psychological resources of intimacy.

SEXUAL ENCOUNTER AND MARRIAGE

Shared sexual experience and genital expression are important contexts for the young adult's development of psychological intimacy. Sexual maturity is reached as one's capacity for mutually satisfying sexual expression with a loved partner is developed and stabilized. "Such experience makes sexuality less obsessive," Erikson remarks. "Before such genital maturity is reached, much of sexual life is the self-seeking, identity-hungry kind; each partner is really trying only to reach himself. Or it remains a kind of genital combat in which each tries to defeat the other" (IYC, p. 137). The experience of sexual play and orgasm in young adulthood can contribute to our willingness to risk self-disclosure, to let down our defenses in the presence of another. Sexual intimacy thus opens out into a larger psychological resource, the "flexible capacity for abandoning [oneself] to sexual and affectual sensations, in a fusion with another individual who is both partner to the sensation and guarantor of one's continuing identity" (ILC, p. 124).

Sexual love is often used as the model and metaphor of human intimacy. The rituals of love-making and the experience of orgasm highlight, in dramatic fashion, features common to other experiences of intimacy as well—the impulse to share oneself with another, the anxious moment of self-revelation, the affirmation of being accepted, the delight in the give-and-take of mutuality. Love-making is a vivid example of the "mutual regulation of complicated patterns" (IYC, p. 137) which Erikson notes as the distinguishing characteristic of intimacy. Sexual love underscores the effect of many experiences of intimacy, to appease the hostilities and conflicts that inevitably arise between persons in close contact. In mature sexual experience the partners achieve a synthesis that overcomes their separateness without diminishing or destroying either. And the conception of new life is a profound sign of the fruitfulness of joint activity and the vitality of intersecting lives.

In our culture marriage is the social paradigm of the achievement of intimacy. Involvement in a heterosexual relationship stabilized in the legal form of marriage is taken as a social sign of adulthood. It also serves as an indication that the intimacy crisis has been, or, more probably, is being, resolved. We all know marriages where the mutuality of intimacy is not achieved, where self-disclosure and empathy play little part. But as a social form marriage demands sharing at many levels of life and self. Goals and aspirations are involved, as well as sexual experience and expression, and one's time and activities. Marriage thus stands as an archetype of the "mutual regulation of complicated patterns" which is the core strength of the psychological resources of intimacy.

The structure of married life—its daily pattern of living, eating, sleeping together—evokes the delights and confusions that are the substance of intimacy. But even at such close quarters these issues can be avoided if they are felt to be too threatening. Thus we find marriages in which little is shared, where even sexual intercourse is disengaged from its attendant impulses toward self-abandonment and mutual care. There are other instances in which marriage may not be about the psychological tasks of intimacy. A couple may publicly enter into a marriage contract and yet not in fact engage in the lengthy and risky process of mutual knowledge and mutual influence that is necessary to establish a new, corporate way of life. For whatever reasons (fear of what this fusion of personalities may entail, or immediate immersion in the absorbing tasks of child-rearing or career development), the couple do not "cleave to

one another" in a full psychological sense. They are living together but have not yet developed a "common life." Another instance is that of young persons who enter marriage as part of an
effort to understand themselves. To a considerable extent adolescent love is an attempt to come to a better sense of identity by
projecting one's diffuse self-image on another and by seeing it thus
reflected and gradually clarified. Marriage in adolescence often has
more to do with these issues of identity than with questions of intimacy. Levinson (1978, p. 107) has noted the peculiar mis-timing,
from a developmental perspective, of marriages which occur
at the very outset of adult life. Often such a "precocious" marriage does not resolve the challenge of intimacy but rather introduces the tasks of this developmental challenge prematurely, before the partners have the resources needed for adult maturity.
Intimacy commitments have a better chance of growth and endurance when they are established on a more stable sense of self and
on a variety of experiences of how a person can be with others
creatively. Thus from his long-term study of "culturally advan-
taged" men Vaillant concludes, "To marry too young, before a capacity for intimacy was developed, boded as poorly for successful
marriage as to exhibit a delayed capacity for intimacy" (1977, p.
216).

Marriage offers vivid examples of intimacy in both its most inviting and its most challenging aspect. But heterosexual marriage
is not the only context for the resolution of the challenge of intimacy. Erikson and other psychologists note that a homosexual
relationship can be a context for the resolution of the intimacy
crisis as well as a sign of this resolution. The possibility of the development of stable homosexual unions is much discussed today by
psychologists, legislators, clergy, and ethicians, as well as by gay
women and men. Many social and psychological pressures exist in
homosexual relationships, complicating their permanence and stability. But, increasingly, heterosexual unions are not free from these
pressures. We can anticipate that the accumulating personal experience of gay men and women as well as continuing research over
the next decades will contribute significantly to our understanding
of the developmental challenges and possibilities of a mature gay
lifestyle.

We also know, from personal experience as well as from the example of mature single and celibate persons, that the develop-

ment of intimacy does not always involve sexual experience or
genital expression. But intimacy does involve real openness, psychological availability to another (and to oneself), a true engagement in which mutuality plays an indispensable part. Mutuality is
an essential element of intimate relationships. Each party is involved both in self-revelation and in responding to the knowledge
one receives from the other. In relationships of full mutuality,
Erikson notes, the sharing goes beyond self-disclosure toward an
interpenetration of lives as "partners depend on each other for the
development of their respective strengths" (IR, p. 231).

CO-OPERATION AND COMPETITION

Experiences of friendship and love are crucial to the full development of a capacity for intimacy. But these are not the only experiences which summon one's resources for being with others.
For the adult, social experiences of co-operation and competition
are important instances of intimacy. Whether in work or play, co-
operation and competition test self-awareness, self-assurance, one's
empathy with others, and the capacity for mutual interaction. Co-
operation involves individuals in joint action to accomplish a common goal. Competition puts individuals in some opposition to
one another in their pursuit of a goal. Both illustrate the essential
elements of intimate relationships. A good co-operator is a person
who is aware of his or her own contribution to the common goal,
both its strengths and limitations; one who is secure enough with
these strengths that they can be made available to the group task,
even in the risk that the contribution may not be accepted; one
who is flexible enough to accept that contribution being modified
by those of others; one with sufficient empathy to rejoice in the
joint accomplishment into which that contribution has been sub-
sumed. The advantages—to oneself and to others—of the development of these intimacy resources make co-operation a valued interpersonal ability. Competition, on the other hand, suffers a bad
reputation. Many therapists, educators, and religious persons share
the conviction that, as much as possible, competition is to be
eliminated in its cultural forms and avoided in one's personal life.
This conviction is born of much experience with the debilitating
effects of competition in the lives of individuals and in the experiences of groups and institutions. Without denying these negative
experiences, we wish to invite a consideration of another aspect of

an admittedly ambiguous phenomenon. Most psychologists today would attest that an ability to compete maturely is an important ingredient of the adult personality. And the psychological characteristics of the mature competitor are remarkably similar to those of the mature co-operator. To compete well—in sports, for example—I must have a realistic sense of my own abilities, with an awareness of both the strong and weak points in my game. Competition forces me to express these abilities, to expose them to the test of a concrete challenge, with the risk that they may not be sufficient. But it is only in taking that risk of failure that I can confirm and develop my strengths. The exchange of competition reveals much about each participant. In the contest I come to a better knowledge of myself and to a special awareness of my opponent. Success in the game is often dependent on flexibility and creativity in modifying myself in response to what I learn about the rival.

These characteristics—awareness of self and other, a sense of self adequate to the demand of mutuality and to the possibility of failure, flexible response to the individuality of other persons—are not germane to sports alone. They are resources that enhance adult personality. These abilities are valuable in a variety of relationships that involve teamwork, advocacy, conflict resolution, negotiation, planning. They are intimacy resources often lacking in persons who cannot—or do not—compete. The developed personality has available a range of psychological resources and a repertoire of varied behaviors. The mature adult is capable of both co-operation and competition and can discern when, and in what combination, each is appropriate.

INSPIRATION AND INTUITION

In his listing of experiences that may evoke in the young adult the developmental crisis of intimacy, Erikson includes inspiration from others and intuitions from the self (IYC, p. 135). These experiences are less obviously interpersonal than friendship and love, co-operation and competition. So they seem less likely as contexts in which the challenge of intimacy may be experienced. A consideration of inspiration and intuition as instances of intimacy adds intriguing nuances to our appreciation of intimacy as a psychological resource. In both there is an experience of receptivity: One receives an idea, one is given an insight, a realization comes unbidden. The new realization can be disturbing. It can raise new possibilities that call into question my established patterns of understanding and action. The example or words of another may invite me to see myself and my situation in a new light. Intuitions from within may alert me to aspects of myself that I have denied or set aside. My identity is challenged. It is this experience of identity questioned, self-definition brought under review, that precipitates the crisis of intimacy. Here one struggles to become intimate with oneself.

If the struggles of my adolescence have left me generally aware and accepting of the strengths, the ambiguities, the contradictions that are a part of me, I can be open in young adulthood to the new information about myself that comes not only as I interact with others but as I grow more sensitive to the world within. Basically accepting of who I know myself to be, I need not defend against other people nor against the impulses of my own soul. This lack of defensiveness frees me to engage in the dialogue of mutual influence that marks adult intimacy.

It is instructive to note the similarities among these social contexts of intimacy we have considered—friendship, marriage, cooperation, competition, inspiration. In each instance there is a revelation of self, some expression or exposure of one's own definition of "who I am." Each involves significant contact with another or, in the instance of one's openness to intuitions, with other aspects of oneself. The other person comes close enough to see, to challenge, to influence my self-understanding. Each is a situation that can generate new information about myself, information which may reinforce or alter some aspect of my identity.

THE STRENGTHS OF INTIMACY

We have seen that the emergence of each new personality resource builds upon strengths acquired earlier and sets the foundation for strengths to emerge later. The new resources for intimacy that are released in the personality in early adulthood build upon the adolescent's resolution of the challenge of identity. If this resolution has been incomplete, the strain that the young adult feels in the attempt to move into intimacy will overcome the impulse toward self-revelation and participation. Where the identity resolution of adolescence has been sound, the young adult can move into those situations which will evoke the resources needed to sustain significant adult relationships. The psychological resources that are developed in the struggle for intimacy include:

—a supple sense of self: I have a basic knowledge and acceptance of myself and yet retain some openness to new information about who I am;

—an empathy with other people and an awareness of their individuality;

—a willingness to be influenced by my awareness of others, an ability to modify myself in response to new information and to the requirements of different interpersonal situations;

—the flexibility to incorporate these modifications into my personality in a way that strengthens rather than diminishes me;

—the creativity which enables me to devise, with other people, patterns of behavior and lifestyle that are mutually enhancing;

—a tolerance for the inevitable strain that is involved in personal accommodation and compromise.

Erikson describes intimacy, considered as a psychological strength of the personality, as "the capacity to commit oneself to concrete affiliations and partnerships and to develop the ethical strength to abide by such commitments, even though they may call for significant sacrifice and compromise" (CS, p. 263). Intimacy is an abiding competence of adult maturity. It is the strength which enables me to commit myself, not to humankind in general or to idealized movements but to particular persons in concrete relationships—aware of the limitation and incompleteness that are involved. Intimacy resources are drawn upon again in living out these commitments. Relationships are not static. People change, and relationships develop over time. Some developments bring the fulfillment of promises and hopes; others make demands for accommodation, for understanding, for tolerance, for forgiveness. A well-developed capacity for intimacy enables a person to honor the promises and demands of commitment and to sustain with integrity the adjustments and compromises required in living with others.

Only with the strength made available in the release of my resources for intimacy can I make the open-ended commitment of loyalty, to do whatever is required to enrich our relationship. Without these resources my impulse toward union will be overcome by a fear of what these commitments may demand in cost to myself. A flexible identity, an empathetic awareness of others, an openness to continued development of the self—these strengths make creative commitment possible.

The person who has responded successfully to the challenges of intimacy is not one who experiences no fear of the loss of self in close contact with others but one who has confronted this fear. Maturity does not eliminate the impulse toward isolation; it puts it in the service of the self. Intimacy and isolation may be seen as poles of a continuum along which relationships fall. The ability to set myself off from others, to be selective in my love, to seek and savor periods of solitude—these are as important indicators of my capacity for adult intimacy as is co-operation or mutual orgasm.

One's lifestyle and commitments can demand the nurturing of some impulses toward intimacy (parents, for example, know that they have to *learn* to love their children) and the inhibiting of others. Selectivity is a characteristic of human love. The sexually active human is not attracted to every physiologically competent partner. Choice is a critical component of adult genital expression. And, as Erikson notes, one's commitments as well as one's preferences are factors in this choice. "A human being should be potentially able to accomplish mutuality of genital orgasm, but he should also be so constituted as to bear a certain amount of frustration in the matter without undue regression wherever emotional preference or considerations of duty and loyalty call for it" (CS, p. 265).

The successful resolution of the intimacy crisis involves the balancing of the positive and negative impulses evoked at this stage of personality development. I struggle toward a personal synthesis which will express this balance of intimacy and isolation in a favorable ratio consistent with my developing personality and appropriate to my lifestyle and commitments. The psychological challenge of young adulthood reaches its resolution in the achievement of this balance. The divergent impulses aroused in the tension of the intimacy crisis are absorbed into a personal synthesis that overcomes these polarities without destroying them. This synthesis emerges in a personally appropriate adult style of intimacy.

The intimacy challenge is not always successfully resolved. Afraid of the risks of close encounter, a young adult may attempt to avoid not only situations in which the challenge of intimacy is obvious (dating and teamwork) but even those contacts with others that might develop toward intimacy (casual acquaintances and social friendships). The adult who has not been able to resolve the opposition between merging with others and defending the self will experience strain in many interpersonal situations. There will be little ability to discriminate among the variety of interpersonal demands made by different situations. One has no range of behavior upon which to draw in responding to different demands. All relationships will seem to ask "too much," to threaten a loss of identity in a fusion of selves. To avoid that frightening possibility, a person may develop a characteristic reserve with others or even seek to avoid many interpersonal situations altogether.

The strain of this interpersonal crisis can provoke three types of avoidance. Each of these inadequate attempts to deal with interpersonal tensions may be experimented with in young adulthood, but they are ultimately inappropriate and unsuccessful. If any of them continues into adulthood as the dominant style of one's interpersonal life, it would be judged immature. These approaches are isolation, stereotyped behavior, and promiscuity. Isolation refers to a sense of *having* to remain alone. I attempt to avoid psychological strain by avoiding many interpersonal situations. This can take the form of physical isolation (I do not spend time with people) or psychological isolation (I am physically present, but not open to relationship). Stereotyped behavior or an overly formal personal style also serves to defend self from the intrusion of others. Little of myself is displayed, at least little of my vulnerability, and not much self-disclosure from the other is invited or allowed. A third response—promiscuity—involves a hectic seeking after intimacy (not always sexual intimacy) in improbable relationships, where circumstances are such that I cannot really share or reveal much of myself.

A failure to develop intimacy relationships with other persons and with one's own inner resources during the critical period of early adulthood may lead a person to settle for highly stereotyped interpersonal relations. Earlier tendencies toward isolation can become, over time, an incapacity to take chances with one's identity and can harden into a general avoidance of any contacts that might lead to intimacy. But such a pattern leads to problems. If not challenged by later successful experiences of intimacy, psychological isolation and self-absorption can become one's adult stance.

Erikson's is a psychosocial theory of development. He understands the movement into a new stage of personality expansion to be influenced by both factors within and factors beyond the individual. And, at least ideally, personal resolution of each new developmental challenge is aided by both internal (psychological) factors and external (social) influences. We have seen above that the issue of intimacy is likely to arise in social situations of co-operation and competition, of friendship, dating, marriage. In these situations my fears and hopes for intimacy must come to terms with society's norms, what my culture has to say about how persons are to be together. My personal style of intimacy has to be worked out in the context of my culture's style of sexual selection and marriage, competition and collaboration. Where cultural norms of intimacy are clear and consistent, the young adult can find institutional supports to help in the achievement of an appropriate personal stance. Our own culture's messages about intimacy, however, are neither clear nor consistent. Faced with ambiguous, often contradictory, norms about sexuality, competition, and mutuality, the young adult often struggles with the intimacy crisis unassisted. As a result she or he can be left with the feeling that decisions concerning these important areas of life are necessarily private and idiosyncratic—that intimacy is simply a personal matter, rather than an important social strength.

INTIMACY AND LOVE

We have mentioned the various social settings which require of the adult a capacity for psychological intimacy. We have discussed the diverse forms of intimate behavior which the adult will need to call upon in order to participate appropriately in the many different roles of family and social life. These include intimacy in friendship, in sexual expression, in collaborative work, in mature competition, in self-knowledge. The most highly developed strength of intimacy to emerge during young adulthood is the love of mutual devotion. A consistent capacity for this kind of love marks one's transition into psychological adulthood. This love moves beyond the energizing but psychologically passive experience of "falling in love" toward a relationship that is chosen and cultivated. Activity and passivity merge in intimate love as each partner engages in the mutual concern of caring and being cared for. Such mutuality endures only if each partner is capable of commitment and of a generous self-disregard. Erikson expresses a conviction shared by those who have been unsuccessful as well as those successful in love: "Only graduation from adolescence permits the development of that intimacy, the selflessness of joined devotion, which anchors love in a mutual commitment" (IR, p. 128). The psychological resources released and strengthened in intimate love enable the partners to develop a way of life in common, one which includes patterns of living, of joint activity, of shared production and even procreation. Our experience of mutual care for each other expands into caring together for what we have produced together. Thus the emergence of the full resources of intimacy in early adulthood already begins to call forth the generativity resources that will reach full development in middle adulthood.

Erikson defines love, this essential psychological strength of young adulthood, as a "mutuality of devotion forever subduing the antagonisms inherent in divided function" (IR, p. 129). Young adults capable of this love have overcome first the internal struggle of their own impulses toward intimacy and toward isolation. In the enduring experience of this love they overcome the antagonisms that, inevitably, develop over time in close relationships. It is the power of this love, the ready availability of these well-developed resources of intimacy, that enables "two people with different histories, divided functions, varying gifts, and unequal powers [to] come together and, in spite of their separateness, mutually activate and mutually affirm" each other (Browning, 1973, p. 153).

This is the power of marriage as a sign and source of love. Marriage can provide the frame within which two persons move toward full and mutual intimacy. Its structure supports the initial risks of self-disclosure and confrontation. Its commitments protect the fragile figure of a developing life-in-common. Its promise of duration invites the open-ended investment that is required for creative (and procreative) activity together. The marriage of mature—or maturing—adults can thus display "that combination (by no means easily acquired, nor easily maintained) of intellectual clarity, sexual maturity, and considerate love, which anchors [men and women] in the actuality of [their] responsibilities" (IR, p. 129).

In relationships of mutuality that endure over time—such as marriage, friendship, or collaboration in work—the continuing reciprocal influence develops into joint activity, which itself often results in some common "work." For a group of friends who engage in recreation together, the result of their joint activity may be simply an enjoyable time for everyone. The efforts of a collaborative team may extend over a longer period of time and result in a common achievement or product. Spouses will effect a shared life; parents will nurture the children born of their love. This impulse toward working together is a natural part of the psychological experience of intimacy. The resolution of the challenge of identity in adolescence leads to a desire to share with another this newly emerging sense of self. As we learn to share ourselves in the mutual regulation of life and activities that is intimacy, we experience the desire to express this mutuality in a common work. And through this common work we are brought to care about and to care for what has been produced. Thus the independent "I am" moves toward the mutual "we are," which itself turns outward as "we care." The products of our creativity challenge us to invest ourselves in their development and well-being. In this challenge we are led toward the next critical period of adult growth—we are invited to generativity.

FOUR

Intimacy and Religious Growth

The heritage of Christianity is rich in religious images and sacred stories. For many of us these images are deep in our consciousness; they express most powerfully the convictions and hopes of our lives. Return now to a religious image that is important for you. What symbol or story or saying comes to you—from the Old or New Testament, from the liturgy—as an image of intimacy. Let the images come as they will: There is no need to "force" one. Wait for one that seems particularly appropriate to you now.

When such an image arises, one that is interesting or even surprising, spend time with it. Be attentive—let it disclose its meaning for you.

After some time, these questions may be helpful:

What in this image confirms your own adult experience of intimacy?

What in the image challenges your own experience of intimacy?

What in the image expresses your hopes for the experience of intimacy in your life?

RELIGIOUS IMAGES OF INTIMACY

Images of intimacy abound in the Old and New Testaments. "A man leaves his father and his mother and cleaves to his wife and they become one flesh" (Gen. 2:24). Provocative sexual imagery appears throughout the Song of Solomon. Images of fidelity and marriage are used frequently to describe the relationship of Yahweh to his people. Another image of religious intimacy, one which captures the threat and ambiguity of such significant encounter, appears in the ancient story of Jacob.

> And Jacob was left alone; and a man wrestled with him until the breaking of the day. When the man saw that he did not prevail against Jacob, he touched the hollow of his thigh; and Jacob's thigh was put out of joint as he wrestled with him. Then he said, "Let me go, for the day is breaking." But Jacob said, "I will not let you go, unless you bless me." And he said to him, "What is your name?" and he said, "Jacob." Then he said, "Your name shall no more be called Jacob, but Israel, for you have striven with God and with men, and have prevailed." Then Jacob asked him, "Tell me, I pray, your name." But he said, "Why is it that you ask my name?" And there he blessed him. So Jacob called the name of the place Peniel, saying, "For I have seen God face to face, and yet my life is preserved." The sun rose upon him as he passed Penuel, limping because of his thigh. Therefore to this day the Israelites do not eat the sinew of the hip which is upon the hollow of the thigh, because he touched the hollow of Jacob's thigh on the sinew of the hip. [Gen. 32:24–32]

It is instructive to examine the elements of this strange story.

The stage is set in the opening words: It is night; Jacob is alone; he is assaulted by an unknown figure. The parallels with the experience of adult crisis are clear. In disorienting darkness one feels beset by an unknown assailant and struggles for one's life. This struggle has its price: "Jacob's thigh was put out of joint as he wrestled with him." As biblical scholar Gerhard von Rad (1961) comments, Jacob "lost something in a very vital spot; and therefore in a certain sense emerged from this struggle broken" (p. 318). In this competitive encounter Jacob is wounded and changed. This threat of loss, the loss of self, stands at the heart of every intimacy crisis. If I give of myself, I may be "taken." I may fall under the other's control or be swallowed up in another's identity. This sense of loss is not unfounded. In the resolution of an intimacy crisis I do give up something of myself. To come to a new, shared identity, some change will be required of me. "I" will be altered in the transition toward "we." The ambiguity and terror of the intimate embrace is that it is uncertain where it will lead: Will I be harmed or healed?

When Jacob asks for a blessing from his combatant, the figure demands to know Jacob's name. This is the demand of any intimate relationship: Disclosure and revelation of self, with all the dangers and potential loss of control that this entails. Jacob gives his name and receives a new name in return. Now he is called Israel. The encounter concludes with Jacob's receiving the figure's blessing. At dawn Jacob limps away, having "prevailed." The limping victor is an apt image of prevailing. Radically different from "conquest," sexual or otherwise, prevailing does not imply domination or control. Success in intimacy, with Yahweh or with fellow humans, is rather a matter of wrestling to a new relationship—one which entails both mutuality and vulnerability. In this relationship, both contestants are altered and yet both prevail. To prevail is to survive the ambiguous embrace, to know it as an embrace of care rather than of control.

The attraction of this story of Jacob wrestling is due, in part, to its ancient form. Von Rad, noting its pre-Israelite origin, refers to the mysterious figure as "this nocturnal assailant [who] was *later considered* to be Yahweh himself, God of heaven and earth, at work with Jacob" (p. 316, our emphasis). This delayed recognition parallels the hindsight with which an adult crisis is often seen to have been a growthful event. Von Rad continues, "Israel has here presented its entire history with God almost prophetically as such a struggle until the breaking of the day" (p. 320). It is not only Israel's experience with Yahweh that is captured in this intriguing story; it describes as well the contemporary believer's intimate relationship with a God whose embrace in the midst of crisis is ambiguously wounding and creative. What begins as an intimidating experience of threat and injury is transformed mysteriously into growth. It is through experiences such as these that we learn, as adults and as believers, the nuances of "prevailing."

MARRIAGE AS A RELIGIOUS
PASSAGE OF INTIMACY

Marriage is for many the crucial transition in early adulthood. The excitement and enthusiasm that attend the beginning of a life together often obscure the difficulty and perils of such a venture. Frequently it is only after time together that the couple recognizes the transition to be a passage of several stages, each of which demands specific strengths and skills. Here we will reflect on marriage as a religious transition and on the specific skills that are tested and (ideally) developed in this passage.

Theologians are often reluctant to explore the Christian sacraments as passages, fearful of an anthropological reductionism that "explains away" the uniqueness of the sacraments. Yet it can be useful to reflect on the sacrament of Christian matrimony in its function as a passage from two independent lives into a new and exciting—but potentially confusing—mutuality. The notion of this sacrament as signaling a developmental passage reminds us that it is dependent on a prior passage—the growth into a somewhat stable sense of identity. A religious insight arising from Erikson's schema is that we should not ask a sacramental passage to resolve at the same time the crises of both identity and intimacy. Some marriages of very young adults, busy about their identity rather than the specific challenges of intimacy, do grow and develop gracefully. But the high incidence of divorce in early-age marriages reminds the Church to be more astute in allowing time for its members to develop the mature sense of self that will give their Christian marriage a better chance to grow.

A second lesson about Christian marriage, explored as a passage, concerns its *gradualness*. The past decade in Catholic thought has seen a significant development away from a legalistic understanding of marriage. This earlier stance stressed the rights enjoyed by the partners and focused on the ritual moment as the transition into the married state. This focus on the sudden realization of moral rights at the moment of the rite of matrimony (what was forbidden until this point now becomes suddenly permitted) led to a neglect of the process of marriage and the stages of the passage into a joint life. An examination of sacraments as passages recovers a more balanced recognition that the ritual celebration of the sacrament must be complemented by a longer process of education, support, and socialization.

The significant transitions of adult life have a duration about them; the passage into marriage takes time. We are reminded, then, that different points in this passage will invite differing responses. At different times the religious community can be called upon to educate, to challenge, to celebrate, and to protect the couple's transition into marriage. Such a passage cannot be accomplished in a single ritual. The sacramental ritual is one of the rites which give shape to the community's response to the dangers and opportunities of the passage into marriage. The sacramental celebration must be embedded in a broader and continuing process of support and challenge. When the sacrament of matrimony is not complemented by such a supportive process, as in the case of couples who want "to be married in church" but who do not plan to involve themselves in Christian life, the sacramental ritual may appear both magical and ineffective.

Religious education, offered in pre-Cana meetings and other marriage preparation programs, is one of the rites of the passage into marriage. Its dual purpose is to share with the couple the religious tradition's wisdom and its hopes for this new stage of life and to provide for them an opportunity to examine the personal strengths and needs they bring to this important transition. Such religious reflection on one's marriage should not end with the marriage ceremony. This sacramental event does not signal that the religious transition has been completed but that it is well begun. Thus the importance of continuing efforts to support couples—through retreats, adult education programming, formation of support groups, marriage encounter, and counseling—in the ongoing religious process of their marriage.

Training in skillful behavior is another rite of passage into marriage. Beyond exhorting the couple to love one another, a believing community can provide training in the specific actions and behavior that demonstrate and foster such love. Skills of mutuality and self-disclosure are especially relevant as means of translating Christian ambitions about marriage into virtuous action.

We have already suggested that the central skill of intimacy is self-disclosure—those attitudes and actions that allow one to be known by others and to know them. Self-disclosure is rooted in self-awareness; it is displayed in listening and assertive behavior

Skills of Self Disclosure

(Egan, 1977). Self-awareness is at the heart of intimacy: I am able to share with another most maturely when I am aware of my own motives and needs and feelings. The skillful minister of marriage, one who is able to assist the broader passage, will give young adults the opportunity to explore the deeper motivations and hopes that are leading them toward this commitment of Christian intimacy. Exercises in self-awareness—journal keeping, guided fantasy, and other methods of experiential learning—will allow both the couple and the Church to determine when the young adults have a firm enough sense of themselves to survive and profit from the challenges of intimacy. Sharing these exercises in awareness can also deepen the couple's understanding of each other, an understanding crucial to this first stage of the passage.

The skills of listening provide the couple the behaviors through which they may demonstrate their understanding and acceptance of each other's hopes and joys as well as their anxiety and apprehensions. The much-talked-of need for communication in marriage is grounded, at least in part, in these skills which assist a person to hear accurately both the ideas and the emotions in the partner's words. It is true that some people seem to be naturally good at listening; but this skill is neither an automatic attribute of all adults nor a gift given mysteriously to a few. We can learn to listen to one another caringly and effectively. An important time for the development of this ability is as one prepares to begin life with another person.

The third element within the larger skill of self-disclosure is assertion. Assertiveness is, as we have observed before, the ability to express one's needs in a fashion that respects both these needs and the other person. As a Christian virtue, assertion lies between the compulsive need to force others and to control situations (aggressiveness) and the inability to communicate one's needs (nonassertiveness). Some marriages, it is true, are unions of an aggressive partner and a nonassertive one. Psychological intimacy is necessarily frustrated in such relationships because of the lack of mutuality. Assertiveness, a skill which seems to come only with some difficulty for Christians, protects the mutuality of intimacy, giving the couple a better chance to grow together instead of separately or even at each other's expense.

The inclusion of these three interpersonal skills within the Church's preparation of couples for marriage will contribute to their growth in intimacy both in their marriage and in their other relationships. These skills might well be included in retreats and renewal seminars where married couples attempt to continue their growth in religious intimacy—with each other and with God.

DISGUISED PASSAGES OF INTIMACY

Marriage, as a crisis of intimacy and as a religious passage, enjoys the advantage of being a scheduled and fully expected event. Adults expect this transition even if they do not anticipate all its inherent challenges. For many Christians today adult life holds other unanticipated and even disguised passages of intimacy. As unscheduled, these transitions have greater likelihood of being experienced as traumatic (Neugarten, 1970). Such critical events present a special challenge to the believing community in its commitment to minister to its members. Here we will discuss two of these disguised passages that are of special relevance to the growth in adult intimacy—the transitions involved in divorce and in "coming out."

DIVORCE

Divorce is an unscheduled crisis of intimacy; adults traditionally enter marriage with expectations of a lifelong relationship. The enormous increase in the incidence of divorce in the past two decades, however, has made it difficult for married couples not to anticipate that such a crisis *could be* part of their own future. Such awareness can lead to quite different responses. For some the prevalence of divorce will lead them to a more circumspect sense of commitment in their own marriage; for others the awareness of divorce will lead to increased efforts to grow in intimacy. The following discussion is meant neither as a defense nor an advocacy of divorce. We begin rather in the fact of divorce as a part of the adult experience of an increasing number of Christians. We will suggest that Christian communities can learn to minister to this crisis more effectively by locating divorce as a crisis of intimacy. The Church's ministry to marriage, the encouragement and education of young adults so that lifelong commitments are possible, must be complemented by a ministry to the divorcing—to Christians who stand in the midst of a specific crisis, one which can be traversed successfully or unsuccessfully, one which requires specific rites of passage and reconciliation.

Divorce, as a legal event, is one resolution of an intimacy crisis (another resolution, of course, being a reconciliation and healing of the crisis within the marriage). As a psychological event, divorce is its own crisis. The dynamic of this psychological crisis is like that of other adult transitions. Peter Marris (1975) draws the parallels between the bereavement following the death of a loved one and the loss experienced in a divorce. The divorcing person may be faced with a similar period of mourning—a time during which he or she must admit the loss and gradually let go of the relationship. Acknowledging the loss demands an accurate acceptance of one's own (though partial) responsibility for it. A mature acceptance of one's own responsibility does not ignore the pain and disruption of the loss. Neither does it rest simplistically in blame or guilt.

The crisis of divorce is negotiated successfully when the person accomplishes this dual task of accepting responsibility and letting go. In the personal reintegration that can follow, the divorced person can emerge with a renewed sense of self as lovable, as still capable of intimacy. The experience of divorce is thus a passage—a dangerous transition from one way of living to another, accomplished by a profound shift in lifestyle and social relationships. The psychological and religious passage of divorce, however, can be disguised by the legal event. Thus a legally divorced person may not yet have navigated the larger passage. Guilt and a sense of failure may cripple a person, inhibiting growth *through* this passage to a next and more mature stage of life. There are signs that the passage has not been negotiated: A recently divorced person rushes into another marriage, to fill the void (and, perhaps, to avoid working through the loss and guilt); another retreats from social life, overwhelmed by this failure and convinced of her or his inability to sustain other intimate relationships. In religiously successful passages adults are able to reconcile themselves with the loss—both accepting responsibility for their contribution to it and learning from it about their strengths and weaknesses. This painful crisis and passage, when successfully traversed, can be expected to leave a person wounded but not crippled—mellowed by the experience and, through it, equipped to be more responsible and caring in relationships.

To this point we have described only the individual in crisis. But we know that individuals are not meant to negotiate such dangerous transitions alone. A person's community and loved ones can be of particular assistance in the time of a divorce, pacing the person through the crisis, helping the person move through the alternative temptations of denial and blame toward a reconciliation of self with God and others in a new stage of life. When we speak of the contribution of the community, we are speaking of the ministry to divorce.

The Church has two distinct ministries to marriage. The first is the ministry of helping adults to grow in the specific virtues (the religiously motivated psychological strengths and interpersonal skills) that will allow the intimacy crises in their marriages to be resolved *within* marriage. The second ministry is to the painful and often traumatic transition of divorce, when it does and must occur.[1] The goal of this ministry is to assist the divorcing or divorced person to discover the special learnings and graces of this difficult time. The awareness of self, of limitation, of sin which characterizes this time need not lead to a destructive sense of failure. These can rather result in growth.

Historically the ministry to divorce within the Catholic Church has been determined by its convictions about the indissolubility of marriage. Although exceptions to this doctrine of indissolubility can be noted (Kelleher, 1976; Noonan, 1972), the Church's traditional stance has been that divorce cannot occur for properly married Christians. With such an understanding predominant, it is not surprising that no direct ministry to divorce has developed. Many priests and other Catholic ministers have been caring and supportive in their own relations with divorcing persons. The Church's official ministry, however, generally has taken one of two forms. The first is denial. To thousands of divorcing Catholics the Church has protested, "This cannot be, is not, happening." The hope in such a ministerial response appears to be that if this crisis is denied, it will not occur. The second response is one of blame. The Church has often accused divorcing persons of failure and convicted them of sin. For persons already quite conscious of failure and of their own responsibility in this loss, such a response

1. Rev. James Young, C.S.P., has been a catalyst in this ministry and in the establishment of the North American Conference of Separated and Divorced Catholics, now headquartered in Boston.

contributed little to the possibility of religious growth through this passage. The effect of these two modes of response has been to reprimand rather than to accompany Christians, with support and challenge, through and beyond this transition.

Both divorce and the subsequent passage of remarriage have seemed intolerable transitions within the Catholic tradition. The decision of the American Catholic hierarchy at the third plenary council of Baltimore in 1884 to excommunicate divorced and remarried Catholics, peculiar as it is in church history, may provide a lead to the source of this understanding of marriage. Excommunication, an ejection from the community of believers, suggests that divorce and remarriage are acts of an "infidel." Such a person is no longer to be included among believers. What is the link in Catholic thought between indissolubility in marriage and fidelity to God?

A clue may be found in one of the most beautiful metaphors in the Judeo-Christian tradition: the marriage relation between Yahweh and Israel. This evocative image captures the unending covenant between God and his chosen people. The dynamic of the relationship is one of human failure, God's forgiveness, and the eventual return of Israel to the bonds of love. Israel's failure was its loss of faith, expressed by Hosea in the powerful image of harlotry. Reconciliation brought Israel back to Yahweh.

This profound metaphor of a faith community's relationship with God came, in time, to be applied to Christian marriage. Here the image is less apt. Chief among its limitations is the likely confusion of a human-with-human relationship with a divine-with-human relationship.[2] Concretely, failure at sustaining a marriage, for whatever reasons, began to be equated with a loss or abandonment of religious faith. Thus divorce and remarriage could appear as comparable to Israel taking up residence with a foreign god. The severity of the Catholic Church's historical position on divorce and remarriage suggests that a confusion of these two levels of commitment and fidelity has not always been avoided. Whether or not rooted in such symbolic confusion, the Church's inability to minister constructively to the divorced and remarried Christian does seem related to a particular understanding of

2. Another limitation is that the man in the relationship tends to be identified with Yahweh, the faithful One, and the woman with Israel, the recidivist harlot.

human growth and change. According to a standard interpretation within Catholic ministry, the only appropriate resolution of a crisis in marriage is reconciliation of the two partners to each other. (Recall the metaphor of Israel and Yahweh: Where else could Israel turn, since the Lord is the true God!) In the many cases where such a reconciliation is simply impossible, the Church's official ministry is either mute or restricted by an essentially non-developmental orientation. For a divorced person to be free to marry again, the previous marriage must be found never to have really existed (annulment).

Here again we see the Church struggle with the reality of change. The full fact of change invites us to re-examine our understanding of commitment and fidelity. We commit ourselves to others, to values, to God. We attempt to live in faithfulness to these commitments in the midst of a changing world, a world in which both we and others continue to grow and change, in which even our perceptions of God change. In the enthusiasm of young adulthood we make vows that are forever. But we cannot always live these out. Sometimes relationships simply die; sometimes they should be brought to an end. In such instances, to cling to a commitment simply because it has been vowed, to remain oblivious to the destructiveness that can attend the relationship in its present form, may be overcommitment rather than fidelity. Fidelity is exercised not only in stability but in change. Married Christians strive to stand together in the necessary and ongoing changes of their marriage. This attempt does not always succeed. There are cases in which fidelity to oneself and to God can be expressed best in acknowledgment that a relationship has died.

Marriages (sometimes) die, but Christian partners survive. The ministerial challenge concerns how they will survive: whether they will have the opportunity to learn from failure, to find—with the help of a community and loved ones—new strengths hidden within this (often) traumatic loss, to discover in the midst of this crisis graces that invite them to go on, to love again, to continue to trust. Such growth can occur if a community can move beyond simply being scandalized by change and give itself both to the effort to witness to its ideals and to care effectively for those who are in crisis. This care, we suggest, might be expressed within the religious community in the development of rites of passage for the divorcing.

RITES OF PASSAGE AT DIVORCE

A first effect of such a rite would be to incorporate the divorcing person within the Christian community, where healing might occur. The experience of personal crisis tends to isolate; the experience of isolation deepens the crisis. This vicious cycle can be broken by my experience of community—persons who do not exclude me (since they are themselves neither afraid nor ashamed of my crisis) but rather hold me in the bonds of relationships, not allowing me to retreat into isolation, self-hatred, or blame. The religious community may structure times in which, with trusted others, I may speak of my grief and mourn my loss. The rites of this passage would thus provide the protective atmosphere in which I may face the disorientation of this period without being destroyed, in which I may attend to my own ambivalence and anger. With this mourning can come both clearer recognition of my own role in the demise of this relationship and an acceptance of its loss. These experiences of community support—both those which are structured and the more informal occasions which arise —invite the divorcing Christian toward a religious reconciliation of an irreversibly terminated marriage. The reconciliation in such a situation is not with one's former partner (at least, not in marriage) but with oneself (a different self, with a new awareness of personal strengths and limitations, hopes and needs) and with God (in a new relationship, forgiven and graced with a new maturity and a cautious hope for the future).

The structured opportunities of a rite of passage also pace a person through the transition and predict a successful outcome. They present the expectation that I can survive this loss and that, gradually, I can recover a sense of self as lovable and capable of intimacy—partly in spite of the divorce and partly because of this powerful experience. The rites of passage promise that through this painful experience I can gain important information about myself and my future, insights and skills that will prepare me for more mature and satisfying relationships in the life that lies ahead for me.

The rites of passage for the divorcing Christian, begun in counseling and continued in a support group, would ideally include an experience of explicit ritual reconciliation—a liturgical event in which the person could acknowledge the resolution of this period of crisis, in the company of those who have been supportive through the passage. Perhaps it must be stated here: Such a celebration is not a means of ignoring the loss or the failure of the divorce. Nor is its intent to make light of the transition or to overlook the personal and social implications of this marriage now come to an end. Quite the contrary, the ritual can provide a means for the community—at least those closest to the individual—to grieve with the divorcing person while anticipating with hope the next stage of life. Soberly yet hopefully, the religious community is thankful for the graces which have seen the person through this passage. Such a ritual is a reconciliation, a reintegration of the divorcing person—now in a new stage of his or her own religious journey—within the community of believers.

Happily, the ministering response described here is beginning to be found in the Church. Though this ministry is still at the margin in many communities, there are creative and caring efforts being made to assist believers through the difficult passage of divorce. Thus is the Church learning, slowly, to respond to the peculiar challenges of this adult crisis. Such a passage will not be traversed automatically or easily; divorce can be an occasion of growth or a frustration of growth. The outcome, often, is related to how well a person's community or loved ones assist in the passage. Rather than simply identifying the divorcing person as a sinner (a designation that, after all, does not distinguish the divorcing person from others in the community!), the Christian community is called to facilitate the passage of divorce when it is the only truly available response to a broken relationship. A recognition of divorce as an adult crisis of intimacy may also assist the Church to deal more effectively with the question of remarriage. Rather than defining the divorced person to be in a terminal state, with return to a former marriage being the only intimacy reconciliation possible, the Church may recognize another reconciliation—that of a person to a new relationship with self and with God. This recognition would allow the Church to be more helpful to those Christians who move from divorce toward another marriage. Such a marriage would not be acceptable only upon the annulment (denial) of the former marriage; it could be recognized as a sincere effort of a Christian—wounded, limited, but redeemed—to take up again a holy life of intimacy in marriage. By learning to minister more effectively at this time of adult transition, the

Church can render its divorced members not merely penitent, but more mature and virtuous—thus able to make a more vital contribution to the building up of the community.

COMING OUT FOR THE GAY CHRISTIAN

Two notes on labels: Words such as "homosexual" or "housewife" or "husband" are commonly used to refer to particular subgroupings of persons. Such categorical labels serve as shorthand and are often helpful in conversation. But their use is not without danger. Categories often result in stereotyping, the tendency to define a person according to one characteristic and to discount other individualizing aspects of the person's life or character.

If the label "homosexual" easily effects an exaggerated concentration on one aspect of a person, it also attempts to describe a range of adults with strikingly different lifestyles and degrees of maturity. There are as many ways to be gay as there are to be straight. Our reflections here have been influenced by a quite specific group of adults: persons in their twenties and thirties who, with maturity and responsibility, are seeking ways to be faithful to whom they know themselves to be—Christians who are gay. It is upon this group of adult believers, so unlike the cultural stereotype of the homosexual man or woman, that this discussion is based. The challenges and confusions concerning homosexuality are manifold; here we offer one interpretation of the course of maturation for the gay adult.

"Coming out of the closet" designates a complex, perilous and, until recently, disguised adult passage. The transition is first one of identity (a passage into self-recognition and acceptance) and then one of intimacy (a passage into a way of being with others). The metaphor of the closet captures both the origin and the necessity of this transition. A closet is a protective environment; well-boundaried and dark, it functions excellently as a hiding place. But a closet is also confining; when one is inside, it is hard to see and almost impossible to communicate. Human growth and religious development invite passage from such costly and limiting protection toward more explicit affirmation of one's identity. Such a passage is prerequisite for growth in intimacy. Three distinct passages seem involved in the gay adult's coming out. These transitions are explored here apart from an explicit consideration of sexual or genital expression.

The interior passage. The initial passage is from ignorance of self and one's sexual identity to awareness and self-acceptance. Because of the cultural and religious unacceptability of homosexuality, a gay person may reach adulthood unable to admit feelings of attraction for persons of the same sex. Confusing emotional responsiveness with external behavior, a gay adult may fear these feelings of warmth and desire for others. If denied, these feelings remain unavailable to the individual. The religious as well as the psychological tragedy of such closeting is that one can make responsible choices about feelings only as they are available and accepted. The interior passage for the gay adult is from self-denial (here in its most ironically unchristian sense) to "self-availability" (Nouwen, 1971). This is a passage of identity, toward a more conscious recognition and more complete acceptance of who one is.

Such a passage can be expected to involve a painful and potentially disruptive crisis. Psychologically it shares the characteristics of other adult crises, although its resolution may be more difficult the later it occurs in the developmental schedule. As in any crisis, the person must decide if the risks (here, loss of the security of the "closet" and loss of anonymity to oneself) are worth it. The alternative to the passage is a choice to remain in the dark—not so much to others as to oneself. The radical denial of self that is required in this choice makes the achievement of mature intimacy with others most unlikely.

Although this is a rather private passage, it is clear that it is best not negotiated alone. A fortunate person will find a friend, a minister, a counselor to assist this interior passage. The stentorian silence of the Church as some of its members attempt this difficult passage does not exemplify how a community is to assist such critical transitions.

The social passage. This second passage, sometimes undertaken simultaneously with the first, is a transition into being known in one's full identity by others. This passage is distinguishable from the first since it is a more social transition and is grounded in the person's need to be known concretely and fully for who he or she is. As a sharing of one's identity, this transition represents a movement of intimacy.

This passage may be attempted and traversed in a variety of social settings. A gay adult may share his or her identity with a few close friends. This relatively private sharing may be complemented by dating and by participating in the social life of gay restaurants and bars. Here the gay adult explores ways of being with others as another person would in a heterosexual singles' bar. The Christian churches are gradually recognizing the need to provide more explicitly religious contexts for the gay adult's growth in social intimacy. Organizations such as Dignity (Roman Catholic) and Integrity (Episcopal) attempt to provide a supportive environment as well as to offer specific workshops and liturgical experiences in which gay Christians may recognize and share themselves with others. These supportive contexts can serve as religious rites of passage for the gay Christian's growth in religious maturity. These rites challenge and complement the secular rites of passage within the subculture of the gay community.

The social passage has much of the threat of the first transition —the risk that sharing one's identity will lead to rejection. It is the self-acceptance and self-love gained in the interior transition that provides the confidence for the gay adult to risk this revelation of self to friends.

The public passage. This third passage or third stage of coming out entails presenting oneself in the public domain as a gay person. A variety of motives may influence this transition. Among these are the desire to be known publicly for who one is and the hope of contributing to a better public understanding of gay life. This second motive, that of contributing to a maturing social understanding of homosexuality, points to the potentially altruistic impulse of such a passage. This third transition is best accomplished by a person who is fortified by the strengths gained in the previous two passages. When this third passage is attempted prematurely—before one has developed much self-acceptance or interpersonal intimacy—a more severe and traumatic crisis can be expected.

The public passage has risks of a different order from the previous two transitions. The possibility of negative social reaction and religious recrimination may argue that a person not attempt to be known publicly as gay. Developmentally this social passage is less imperative than the previous two, since the earlier movements can provide the self-acceptance and psychological intimacy most crucial to an effective and holy adult life.

The fundamental issue in all three passages is not one of sexual or genital expression. The Christian community, for example, has many celibate gay ministers and priests who have long given mature and selfless service. The issue is the need of every adult to come to self-acceptance and a life of self-giving that is mature and fulfilling. The challenge is the development of rites of passage through which the Church can assist its members, gay and straight, to make the transitions that are required for development as mature Christians. Religious communities that refuse to explore, concretely and openly, the challenges of gay Christian life are refusing to assist the religious growth of their gay members. In so doing, they deny the larger community the benefit of the religious gifts and insights with which its gay members have been graced.

Discussion and debate will continue concerning the meaning, origins, and morality of homosexuality.[3] Exhortations to orthodoxy (whether doctrinal, scriptural, or psychoanalytic) will, ultimately, be less instructive than the patient witness of orthopraxy —the mature, holy lives of gay Christians. Whether and how "gay is good" will be learned here, but only by the believing community which has developed the skills to observe and the courage to be taught.

SELF-INTIMACY

A challenge of adult growth is to come to a greater awareness of and comfort with oneself. Adults experience themselves not as simple individuals but as complex combinations of different and often conflicting desires, fears, and motivations. Psychological development as well as religious growth has as one of its goals a harmonizing of these disparate parts of the self. This is not simply a private or narcissistic task, since it is in our loving and working with others that we are confronted with those different facets of ourselves that invite greater integration.

This developmental task we can describe as that of self-intimacy. Beginning in the challenge to attend to "intuitions from the recesses of the self" (Erikson, CS, p. 264), the goal of this

3. Among the prolific literature now appearing on this question, one might consult Gregory Baum's article "Catholic Homosexuals" (1974); Donald Goergen's *The Sexual Celibate* (1974); John McNeill's *The Church and the Homosexual* (1976); and Patrick Henry's "Homosexuals: Identity and Dignity" (1976).

effort is the development of an increased awareness and comfort with one's feelings, ambitions, and motives. This awareness is the basis of conscience, described by Erikson as "that dependence on [oneself] which will make [one], in turn, dependable" (CS, p. 405).

The self-intimacy to be achieved is a two-directional awareness: recognition of the multiple movements within the self at present, and a recovery of the influential forces in one's past. An increased awareness of the self means greater understanding of the convictions and impulses which influence one's present. Recurring daydreams and surprising surges of apprehension or anger offer important information here. Such information can be ignored; anxiety or dissipation can distract us from its meaning. But attention to these sources of self-knowledge is an important part of a contemporary Christian spirituality.

The second focus of self-intimacy is one's past. For most adults the personal past is a dense accumulation, rich with significant persons, partially understood events, and still-hidden motives. Adults are seldom intimate, or even familiar, with this personal past. Frequently the significant events of the last ten or twenty years, events which shaped and continue to influence one's present, are not easily available to memory. These incidents, occurring in periods of turmoil or failure or exhilaration, are often so emotionally charged that they cannot be understood fully as they happen. Only with time and distance can one return to them to integrate their meaning into the present. It is this intentional return to the past, with the goal of a recovery of the learnings and graces buried in these events, that we will explore here.

The past is important, psychologically and religiously, because it holds a wealth of information useful not only for private reverie but for one's loving and effective participation with others. Psychiatrist Robert Coles has observed the importance of a recovery of the past within his profession: "I suppose that is what psychoanalysis at its best can sometimes do, help people live intimately enough with their past to learn how to use its power, not simply to know the details" (1966, p. 164). The past does not "explain" the present; rather it functions as an important resource to one's present growth. But the past can contribute its power to the present only when it has been befriended and healed. This befriending and healing of the past are the actions of self-intimacy.

Two psychological perspectives on this intimacy with one's past are of interest here. Don Browning (1973) suggests that the ability to return to the personal past and to employ it as a resource for growth and re-creation is a characteristic of the mature person. Browning alludes to the playfulness of such a return, a playfulness which he likens (p. 197) to Ernst Kris's "regression in service of the ego." Such a "regression" to the past is healthy when it leads to a greater integration in the present of the strengths and weaknesses of one's past. The playful aspect of this return points to a mature person's comfort with the past and also to the important role of imagination in allowing access to this dense and exciting realm. There is also evidence to suggest that the experience of being a parent may facilitate this growth in self-intimacy. A parent's association with a child invites a recollection of the adult's own childhood in ways that can be regenerative (Benedek, 1959). Gould suggests the dynamic that is involved: "The parent is capable of structural change because in the deep part of his mind the experiences he has with his child are opportunities to rework . . . memories of his own childhood. This is made possible by a kind of limited regression and emotional symbiosis on the part of the adult parent to the level of the developing child" (1972, p. 522). In both instances recovery of the past is a condition for its healing.

Self-intimacy is also clearly a religious task. For a believer the personal past is a deposit of faith and a history of salvation. The achievements, confusions, and failures that in part make up this past hold information about one's intimate relationship with God —information not fully grasped in the density and complexity of these events as they occurred. Christians return to their past in acts of religious recollection or *anamnesis*. Convinced that their present life is empowered by the events and encounters that have gone before, Christians have always exercised themselves in recalling, in making present, the salvific acts of the past. The Church sustains and increases its intimacy with Jesus Christ in celebrating the Eucharist "in memory of" him. Religious education fails when its empowering recovery of the past is limited to events in the life of Israel or of Jesus and the early Church, to the neglect of the concrete personal histories of individual believers in the present.

The personal past often remains relatively hidden or forgotten by an individual because it holds failure and unforgiven injuries. Psychological maturity and religious growth both invite the adult

to return to these painful events with the intent of reconciliation.
Whether the event was a self-inflicted wound or a suffering received undeservedly from another, the adult can return to it, heal
it, and thus diffuse its negative force. This "healing of memories"
(Linn and Linn, 1974) is both a psychological and a religious act.
As a psychological task, this healing of memories appears to reach
critical importance in one's early forties. As we shall examine in
the chapters ahead, increased interiority and a deeper appreciation
of limitations—one's own and others—contribute to the need and
ability for such growth in self-intimacy at mid-life. For the Christian, the ability to forgive[4] oneself and others comes as a surprise
and gift; it is recognized as a grace from God. The sacrament of
penance and the recently revised rite of reconciliation have such
forgiveness as their goal. The practice of confession falls out of
use (as it has in many places today) when guilt and ritual repetition replace self-intimacy as the psychological ground of this religious exercise.

The result of such reconciliation is often that this painful or
hated part of my past is emptied of its power over my present. Accepted and forgiven, this past event need no longer crowd compul-
sively into my life today. Rather it can become truly *past*. The
past is thus healed: Neither denied nor glorified, it no longer in-
trudes into the present as obsession or nostalgia but contributes to
a new depth of self-understanding which mature adults enjoy.
More powerfully in touch with who they are, such adults can better invest themselves in the generative and caring activities of
their life.

One of the goals of a contemporary Christian spirituality will
be to facilitate self-intimacy. A ministry to this religious intimacy
will provide—in prayer, in the liturgy, in support groups—opportunities for exercises of reconciliation with oneself. Christian
adults will be challenged to develop lifestyles that permit such
reflectiveness; they will be encouraged to expect in their recollection the healing presence of God. For it is adults who discern
the patterns of God's action in their own past who can most fully
appreciate this gracious presence in their life today.

4. Tom Driver (1974) argues that when one is attempting a reconciliation
with a previously rejected or hated part of oneself, the healing is better
effected by loving than by forgiving. The rejected part of oneself does not so
much ask for a condescending forgiveness, but asks to be loved, to be attended
to and embraced.

FIVE

The Invitations
of the Mid-years

Adulthood is a time of personal power. As we move into a consideration of the challenges and potential of the middle adult years, first take time to locate yourself. Consider your own recent experience of competence and success—in your work or your community, as parent or as volunteer, as leader or as follower. Let your memory play over the various situations of the past few months or the past year in which you have felt yourself to be effective. Take several minutes for this, letting yourself dwell on these experiences of success.

Now, select from among these one instance of your competence or personal power. Spend time with its memory. Let it take shape and become rich again with detail. What was the occasion? What did you do? Who was with you? How did it turn out? Spend the time to allow the experience to become real again for you.

As you consider this experience of yourself as an effective adult, consider these questions and the thoughts and feelings they evoke:

What does this experience say to you about who you are? How does it contribute to your sense of yourself?

Has it anything to say to you about the ways in which you are engaged with other people, involved with other adults?

What does it say to you about the direction or focus of your life?

There are many ways to look at the broad scope of human experience between the thirties and the sixties. Some developmental psychologists suggest three phases of middle adulthood, roughly coinciding with each age decade (Vaillant, 1977). Others single out a particular age as signaling the onset of a mid-life transition (Levinson, 1978). Some would hold that the experience of adults is so diverse that these attempts to generalize are premature. There is agreement about the issues that are of vital concern in the mid-years—career development and consolidation, concern for adolescent and adult children, reassessment of commitments and accomplishments, responsibility for aging parents, recognition of the inevitability of one's aging and death. There is less agreement about the universality, the timing, and the sequence of these concerns.

Our discussion of middle adulthood here will follow Erikson's lead. Recognizing the diversity in individual experience during this time, we will nevertheless consider these central years of adulthood together under the notion of generativity. The interests and concerns that dominate the middle period of adult life raise a new psychological challenge. I become a participant in a larger social world and must determine the ways in which I will respond to its needs and invitations. I experience the chance to assume a powerful and productive presence in my world both as an opportunity and as a demand. I test my personal resources—my talent, vision, courage.

This challenge arises in part from changes within myself and in part from the demands of new social roles. I move into my thirties with a growing sense of my own effectiveness and a desire to use this personal power in order to assume leadership and act in the world. Social factors reinforce these impulses. As a parent I have immediate and concrete responsibilities for the lives of other people. As worker, volunteer, colleague, householder, citizen, I am involved with others in networks of mutual expectation and reciprocal action.

PSYCHOLOGICAL ISSUES AT MID-LIFE

Psychologically the mid-years are marked by the dominance of three interwoven themes: personal power, care, and interiority.

Personal power. The middle-aged person wants to be, needs to be, effective in the tasks that define her or his work. Competence and experience combine to place the middle-aged in positions of authority. The desire for responsibility, willingness to assume leadership, an ability to take control are important motivating factors in middle age. They create channels through which one's personal power is both manifested and put in the service of a larger social world.

Care. The middle-aged person wants to be, needs to be, responsible for others. The mature person "needs to be needed." Much of the competence and power of the middle-aged is focused in nurturance—of one's children, of younger colleagues, of clients, of an institution or project or plan. The commitments of the middle-aged often make altruism, the unselfish service of the welfare of others, a necessity. Their psychological resources make such generous concern a real possibility.

Interiority. The outward movement of expanding responsibility in the mid-years is accompanied by a movement within. There is heightened sensitivity to the self and an increasing focus on inner needs. Personal commitments seem to demand re-examination and values are reassessed. For some this new introversion is frightening. It is experienced as "middle-aged depression," and attempts are made to avoid it. Others welcome it as a new, or reawakened, experience of their interior life.

It is in the interplay of these three dynamics—personal power, care, and interiority—that the challenges of the mid-years are experienced. As we look more closely at each of these challenges, we shall supplement Erikson's developmental perspective by reference to the work of Bernice Neugarten at the University of Chicago, George Vaillant at Harvard, Marjorie Fiske Lowenthal and her colleagues at the University of California, and Daniel Levinson at Yale.

PERSONAL POWER IN ADULTHOOD

Growth through adult life is not achieved in neatly demarcated units. We are summoned to new matters of maturity while still engaged with earlier issues. Throughout adult life, Erikson remarks, "all persons can be seen to oscillate between at least two stages and move more definitely into a higher one only when an even higher one begins to determine the interplay" (DBL, p. 25). Thus in the first phase of adult life[1] a person can be expected to be working on a resolution of the challenges of intimacy while preparing for the soon-to-be-confronted tasks of generativity.

The young adult is perhaps best described as energetically involved in self-expression—a self-expression which deals both with intimacy and, in a preparatory fashion, with the tasks of generativity. This self-expression is exercised in interpersonal relationships in which the person tests and develops the ability to be with others and to commit the self in a special way to some few of these others. Whether already married, preparing for marriage, or having chosen not to marry, the individual is involved in learning about others—whether and to what extent his or her identity can be risked in drawing close to them.

The other mode of self-expression in young adulthood, that of greatest interest here, leads to one's initial job or career choices. Contrary to some cultural expectations that young adults should "get a job and settle down," Levinson found career commitments in the first stage of adult life to be quite exploratory and provisional. Careers do not begin abruptly or definitively. In initial job experiences a young adult explores the personal ideals that were developed in adolescence. These ideals (whose earliest formulations were in the shape of the child's ambition to be a fireman or a nurse or a doctor) are now tentatively tested in the nonfantasy

1. The boundaries of this period vary greatly. For some it begins before twenty with marriage and one's first job; for others, years of education effect a moratorium, delaying entry into the tasks of young adulthood. Levinson delineates a period of "entering the adult world (23–28)" (pp. 78–84) which can, for shorthand purposes, be taken as the first stage of adulthood. Lowenthal et al. (1976) examined persons at four stages of adult growth. The second of these categories, consisting of a group of young adults in the first year of marriage and just embarking on careers, is also representative of this period.

world. False starts and disappointments are to be expected as one learns the range of personal competencies and the concrete possibilities for being creative and generative in the world in which one's life is lived. Levinson examined the careers of four groups of men—laborers, businessmen, biologists, and writers. Within each group he found job movement and career confusion through the twenties. The biologists, generally, had not settled on a science career until their late twenties. The writers worked at many jobs in their twenties as they tested the viability of an artistic career. Successful growth into generativity appears to depend, often, on such exploratory and provisional periods during which young adults are allowed to test out, with the false starts and failures that are implied, their own potential and competence.

Levinson discusses two ways in which young adults explore their productivity and creativity: in developing the dream, and in forming mentor relationships. The "dream" represents that vision or ambition of what the young adult might do with his or her life. Necessarily idealistic, the dream is an inner suggestion of an occupation or career or vocation. There are two ways in which this dream is intimately related to growth in generativity. First steps into productivity and achievement frequently are guided by and represent a testing of this dream. And the mid-life transition of the early forties often includes an attempt to re-evaluate one's dream and thus to come to a new sense of this deepest ambition and personal vision. Tentative explorations of the dream in early adulthood, explorations crucial to its later expression in one's career, can be frustrated in a variety of ways. I may find myself moving toward a career that represents my parents' dream for me more than my own. Or early marriage and family responsibilities may seem to close my options prematurely, making it difficult for me to take the risks involved in exploring my dream. Sometimes choices of marriage, family, and career reflect the expectations of one's culture or family more than personal decision. To the extent that such choices ignore deep instincts and ambitions of the person, the mid-life transition will be more severe.

While the first stage of adult life is a time for testing the dream, it is also a period in which the person may be involved in an enterprise that combines tasks of intimacy and generativity: finding a mentor. A mentor is an older person who can guide and support me in my initial efforts to establish a career and become an independent adult (Levinson, pp. 97 ff.). A mentor is both a sponsor and a friend, one who supports and facilitates the early efforts to realize the dream. Such a person champions the young adult and, often, models an effective style of adult living and working.

Many young adults, of course, do not enjoy such mentors. Some simply have no sustained contact with older persons; others have older colleagues who intimidate and control instead of encouraging and nurturing them. In general, women are especially lacking in mentors. There are few older women who function for them as role models and even fewer older men who can nurture their careers in a respectful and noncontrolling fashion.

The role of mentor combines, as we have noted, opportunities for both intimacy and generativity. Levinson observes that "mentoring is best understood as a form of love relationship" (p. 100). Perhaps a special value of such a relationship is that it offers a model of adult intimacy that is nonsexual. Neither a parent nor a lover, the mentor presents an alternate model of adult intimacy. Having a mentor thus invites growth in the capacity for intimacy. This intergenerational relationship is also allied to the challenges of generativity. The relationship can be seen as that of older colleague and apprentice; in the initial expressions of his or her own creativity, the younger person enjoys the supervision of an experienced associate and friend. This supervision is, however, not only a business relationship. It is an overseeing by someone interested both in the person's work and in the person.

The mentor is a transitional figure in the life of the young adult. Without the control or authority of a parent, the mentor invites a young person to fuller self-expression both in work and in personal relationships. This invitation, however, is ambiguous. After some years of developing intimacy and colleagueship in the mentoring relationship, Levinson indicates, the younger person will need to separate from the mentor, often with considerable distress to each party. The distress of the separation, which parallels the separation from one's parents, is often surprising and embarrassing, coming as it does in one's adulthood rather than in adolescence.

In summary, the earliest stage of adult life, often associated with the twenties, is a time characterized by energetic self-expression. I am forming the intimate relationships that will issue in personal creativity and family; I am exploring a career, often with great exuberance and confidence (Lowenthal et al., 1976, p. 70). If

adult development is understood as growth in personal power from
productivity and creativity toward generativity, then the first stage
of adulthood is focused most emphatically on productivity—self-
expression in its most active and, often, least reflective form.
Such self-expression and the development of personal power is an
important preparation for the later challenges of generativity.
What I create, in family and in work, during this period is what I
will be asked to be responsible for in the coming periods of adult
life. The opportunity to explore my potential, guided by a dream
and sustained by a nurturing mentor, provides the preparation for
the tasks of middle adulthood.

THE EXPERIENCE OF MIDDLE AGE

It can be misleading to assign a particular age as the beginning
of the psychological stage of middle adulthood. But there are experiences which signal the transition. For some middle age begins
in the realization that there is "nobody here but us." This realization can be disconcerting. Confronted with the dilemmas of
adulthood, it is comforting to think that someone knows an answer, can see a way through, has a plan that will work unambiguously. Coming to maturity in middle age often involves a recognition that there are few unambiguous answers, that adult
decisions are as often made in the face of contradictions as in response to certitude. The realization that, in most of the significant
questions of life and in many of the ordinary ones, no one knows
any more than I do, is a harbinger of the mid-years.

Adulthood is marked by a gradual increase in one's awareness of
personal impact on and effectiveness within one's world. Adults
know themselves to be agents and initiators. A first realization
that "I can make a difference" is part of the exuberance of the
young adult. With middle adulthood comes the awareness that
this personal agency is accompanied by personal responsibility.
Both accountability (I am responsible for what I have done) and
care (I have responsibility for what I have created) come into perspective.

It is in the mid-years that one is conscious of being a member
of the generation now in charge. It is myself and people like me
who are in control. I am no longer in the generation being so-
cialized; I am a member of the generation which is socializing

others—as parents, employers, teachers, legislators. In family life the middle-aged are the generation-in-between, feeling responsibility for both aging parents and adolescent children. The older generation is no longer a protective buffer between self and the demands and absurdities of existence. In middle age, as parents age and die, death becomes a real possibility for oneself.

Changes in the sense of time and the sense of self are characteristic of the transition into mid-adulthood. There is a shift in the mid-years to thinking of my age as time-left-to-live more than as time-since-birth. This is accompanied by an awareness that my past cannot be changed and that my future is not open to all possibilities. The self-consciousness of the teen-ager and the sometimes cocky self-confidence of the young adult are transmuted in middle age into a clearer sense of both my abilities and my limitations. Bernice Neugarten (1970) speaks of the "self-utilization" of middle adulthood, as the individual becomes aware that "I am the principal agent of my life." I "use" myself—my abilities and limitations—in a more conscious and deliberate way, knowing that my own actions and choices will influence significantly the contexts in which my life is lived out.

THE CHALLENGE OF GENERATIVE CARE

Early in adulthood, as we have noted, there are intimations of generativity in one's attempts to accept responsibility, to meet the demands of the workplace, to measure oneself against the tasks of being a productive adult. In their thirties most adults are busily involved in an effort which Vaillant calls "career consolidation." Characteristically, men at this stage are preoccupied with their work; they can be unreflective, even dull (Vaillant, p. 218). Many women, whether or not they work outside the home, are absorbed in the most active phases of parenting, with much physical and emotional energy focused on their children. Levinson designated this period as the time of "settling down" (p. 139). I may begin to experience an intermediate phase of the generativity challenge —a movement beyond productivity toward creativity. Having come to a sense that I am adequate to the basic demands of my adult responsibilities, I can be moved by the desire to be creative. I want my work to bear the stamp of my own individuality, the mark of my own distinctive set of talents and experiences. Knowing that I *can* work, I now want my work to say "me."

But creativity is not yet generativity. The challenge of the generative stage is not only "Can I, will I produce in the larger social world?"—not even "Can I, will I be creative in my productivity?" The generativity question is "Can I, will I be responsible in nurturing life?" The earliest impulse toward productivity is often influenced by social expectations, the desire to prove myself adequate. The intermediate impulse toward creativity is often influenced by a desire for self-expression, to give personal shape and definition to what I do. The impulse of generativity takes its strongest cue from the needs of that which has been produced. Generativity absorbs (but does not do away with) the impulses to prove myself and to express myself, into the capacity to give of myself.

For Erikson, this is the developmental movement into generativity (CS, p. 267). The ability to be intimate, in genital love or in co-operative work, has productive result. That which has been produced—a child, a plan—stands in the world in its own right. But this new life may well die unless it is nurtured. The development of generativity charts the expansion of one's emotional life to include concern and care for what one has made. Generativity describes an attitude toward one's power and productivity and toward what this power has produced. It issues in behavior that is both responsive and responsible.

As marriage does for intimacy, parenthood serves as a central instance of generativity. Giving birth and caring for one's own children is a dramatic experience of generative adulthood. In being a parent one experiences a full range of the delights and demands that accompany a creative, responsible presence in the world. The birth of a child commits parents to a broad range of responsibilities the impact of which they cannot fully predict.

Parents must learn to deal respectfully with dependence. They must first be willing to accept the radical dependence of the infant and the young child, not shying away from the weight of its demands. They must learn to be dependable in ways that neither betray nor exploit this vulnerability. And finally they must nurture the child's movement away from dependence upon them into autonomous adulthood.

For Erikson, "generativity is primarily the concern for establishing and guiding the next generation" (IYC, p. 138). This concern derives its vitality from "man's love for his works and ideas as well as for his children." And while "parenthood is, for most, the first, and for many, the prime generative encounter, yet the perpetuation of mankind challenges the generative ingenuity of workers and thinkers of many kinds" (IR, p. 130–31). Thus parenthood serves as a model for generativity in that it manifests dramatically many elements of the larger psychological challenge. But biological parenthood is not a guarantee of psychological capacity for responsible adulthood, and neither is childlessness an insurmountable barrier. There are many experiences in adulthood that raise the question of personal power or test my capacity for responsibility and care. Both a new career opportunity and a job loss can invite a re-examination of my productive involvement in society. Either the success or the failure of a project that is "my baby" can lead me to a new sense of responsibility for what I do. Clients or colleagues may test my capacity for altruistic concern even more than my children.

Generativity points to a willingness to use my power responsibly in the service of interests that go beyond myself. Thus a chief effect of the successful transition into the mid-years is the expansion of the capacity to care. As I mature as an adult, the boundaries of what really matters to me expand to include more than those things that touch my own life. My sense of responsibility for the well-being of what I have created may lead to a personal investment in broader social concerns: not just improving my child's classroom, but working for a better educational system; not just keeping property values stable in my neighborhood, but planning for better local land use. Signs of mature generativity emerge in my concern for the well-being of a world that will outlive me. I am willing to spend my personal power and social influence in the purchase of a future that is "better," even though I may not live to see the results.

It is not until one has accumulated the psychological resources and social experience of the middle-aged adult that such genuinely unselfcentered devotion to the well-being of others can be sustained with consistency. This mature capacity for care includes an ability to make an emotional investment in the life of what I have created, not just as an extension of myself but according to its own requirements. Not until I experience this demand for the unselfish support of a life or work that has an impetus of its own is the challenge of generativity faced. The invitation is to foster life —to continue to invest myself as my involvement is guided less and less by my needs and more and more by the demands of the new life itself. I am able to resist the impulse to repudiate the new life angrily or bitterly when it begins to demand its independence. Rather I struggle to learn how to "hold on" appropriately as long as needed and how to "let go" appropriately as soon as needed. This tension may be experienced in the family, as I release my children into independent adulthood; it may be experienced in my work, as both projects and junior colleagues move out on their own.

The challenge of generativity thus marks a critical time in an adult's life, a turning point in personality development. If the transition is accepted and well-navigated, I am enriched by new psychological resources that make possible my effective and generous engagement in the world. But the transition can fail. I may be afraid to test myself in the public arena. I may be reluctant to move beyond the security of my intimate world. I may see my children or the works of my hands as possessions or simply as confirming signs of my own worth. I may resist the demands and inconveniences of social responsibility. I may be unable to nurture without control. Erikson alerts us to the debilitating effects of the failure of generativity. "Where such enrichment fails altogether, regression to an obsessive need for pseudo-intimacy takes place, often with a pervading sense of stagnation and personal impoverishment" (CS, p. 267). If fear or self-centeredness blocks my impulse to participate in the social world, the result can be growing self-absorption. The resources of personality appropriate to this stage of adult maturity become atrophied and a sense of boredom and personal stagnation can result.

We see here the relationship between generativity and personal power. My capacity for care is rooted in my awareness of personal power. It is this power that I use, I spend, I "give away" as I care for others. But to be truly able to care is to be conscious of the limits of my own power. And one of the ambiguous fruits of the movement into middle age is an awareness of these limits. Gone is the illusion that I can control my world; I am less susceptible to the deception that I can "save" myself or those whom I love. Life remains a mystery: I am not privy to its secrets, I have not mastered its design. "What is best" does not reside solely within my view. I am humbled by this realization, but I am also relieved. And I am better able to care without always needing to control. Care, notes Sennett, is "a product of learning human limits, learning the limits of a person's concern and power in the world" (1970, p. 121). And "to be responsible as an adult means to champion a person or thing without feeling responsible for its destiny" (p. 126).

The successful movement into generative middle age will be characterized by the development of a personally appropriate style of social involvement. For some the range of this involvement in creating a better world will extend primarily to "my children and my children's children." Others may encompass a commitment to the needs of a broad range of people (one's students or clients or nation), or even an active devotion to the future of humankind. Each of these commitments can provide opportunities in which my strengths and talents will be tested, strengthened, and then gradually moderated by a sense of personal responsibility and by the challenge of generative care.

In his discussion of care, Erikson touches on two paradoxes of generative adulthood—that a key form of the "mastery" that characterizes adult maturity is one of acceptance rather than initiation, and that the shape of adult maturity is dependent upon what one cares for. Adult maturity is not characterized only by initiation and choice. An awareness of my own limits, an acceptance of the givens of life, and a willingness to incorporate these into my subsequent choices and lifestyle—these also are instances of maturity. Often it seems that in the significant areas of adult life—in marriage, family, career, health, friendship—the demand for creative acceptance is as great as that for active choice. Dominance, initiation, and control are valuable qualities. An adult should be able to determine when such assertive behaviors are useful and be able to engage in them appropriately. But these dominant styles may be illusions of maturity if they are the only behavior the adult knows. Much of maturity seems to involve little of personal control. I do not simply choose *ab nihilo* what I will care for or how I will be required to care. There is givenness, even inevitability, in many of the responsibilities of adulthood. A significant part of adult maturity involves coming to terms with this givenness, accepting responsibility in situations and for people that one has not chosen.

"Dependency and maturity are reciprocal," Erikson advises, and "maturity is guided by the nature of that which must be cared for" (IYC, p. 138). In another place he states that "maturity needs guidance as well as encouragement from what has been produced" (CS, p. 267). The development of maturity, thus, is a communal event. In order to mature, I must have the experience of other people being dependent on me. It is in response to other's dependence upon me that I move toward dependability. "Dependents" (children as well as adults in many aspects of their lives) learn how to rely on others through experiences of being dependent upon a mature person, one who does not "use" their vulnerability, one who does not need to keep others subservient or to extend their dependence into other areas of life. But the mature person also needs guidance. I learn how to care by coming to know the inherent needs of what I have produced. My mission in life becomes clearer to me in part as I am willing to be saddled by the responsibilities that come—even without my full intention, even somewhat against my will—by my action in the world. "What has been produced and must be taken care of" guides the development of the adult personality. The dependence of that for which I am responsible provokes, encourages, and shapes my maturity.

INTERIORITY AND THE MID-LIFE TRANSITION

At a certain stage of development (for many, in their early forties) adults begin to experience an increased sense of interiority. This is signaled in a growing emphasis on "introspection and stock-taking," which, Neugarten suggests, is to "be regarded as one of the 'inner' psychological regularities of the life cycle" (1970, p. 77). Vaillant summarizes this shift in the subjects of his study: "At age forty—give or take as much as a decade—men leave the compulsive, unreflective busy work of their occupational apprenticeship, and once more become explorers of the world within" (p. 220).

This often quite sudden change in the maturing adult is related to a number of internal and external events. By forty an adult is usually established in a career; advancement has begun to level off, inviting reflection on what has been achieved and what remains possible in the coming years. Children will be leaving home or are at least relatively independent. These events lead to an assessment of the strengths and limitations of one's relationships and accomplishments. The realization comes that, in Vaillant's felicitous phrase, there are "more yesterdays than tomorrows." This shift in time perspective, well noted in life-cycle research, adds urgency to the task of reflection and interiority at this point in life.

Lowenthal and her colleagues (1976) found that the middle-aged women of their study were experiencing "heightened marital dissatisfaction" (p. 43). This distress and restlessness were not symptoms, as myth would have it, of menopause or the last child's leaving home.[2] They centered on broader questions of intimacy and generativity. The larger issue faced by many married women in their forties is the challenge to focus their generative and nurturing energies in new directions. The symbolic transitions of menopause or the "empty nest" are likely to become a crisis in the dramatic sense only for a woman who has identified her generativity exclusively with family and its maintenance.

This period of change in the early forties, which Levinson labels the "mid-life transition," can also be understood as a crisis of limits (Zullo, 1977). Crisis here does not necessarily refer to a traumatic event but is to be understood in the wider, Eriksonian sense as a period of evaluation and decision. Increased interiority invites me to reflect on the limits of what I have achieved and what I still can do. A new awareness of the limited time left to my life reminds me of my own mortality. This crisis represents not so much a preoccupation with death[3] as a dis-ease with the

2. Lowenthal and Chiriboga (1972) and Neugarten (1970) have found that most middle-aged women meet these two transitions with little distress, since these are scheduled and expected events. Most women, in fact, experienced a "higher level of life satisfaction" during these times (Neugarten, p. 82).

3. Vaillant (p. 220) criticizes Jaques's (1973) emphasis on acceptance of one's mortality as the central task of the mid-life crisis. Mortality is certainly the ultimate experience of limitation but does not predominate in the mid-life transition to the extent that Jaques suggests. It is not irrelevant that Jaques's influential discussion focused upon a psychohistorical analysis of artists.

limitations of what I have done, in the face of a more intense recollection of what I had once hoped to do. The distress of this
time is less often a sign of breakdown and more frequently an
effort to break through the self-imposed limits of one's choices,
while coming to terms with less changeable results of one's history. Vaillant points to this positive aspect of this potentially
disruptive period: "Thus, if men in their forties are depressed, it is
because they are confronted by instinctual reawakening and because they are more honestly able to acknowledge their own pain.
It is not because they fear death. If they are no longer satisfied
with their careers, it may be because they wish to be of more service to those around them. If their marriages are sometimes in
disarray and their groping toward love seems adolescent, it may be
because they are less inhibited than they were in their thirties" (p.
222).

This crisis of limits has as its task, in Levinson's vocabulary,
"de-illusionment" (p. 193). If illusions have been useful, in some
instances, to protect and encourage the young adult, the maturing
person is invited to come to terms with them more realistically.
Nor is this only a negative, painful process: "A man may feel
bereft and have the experience of suffering an irreparable loss. He
may also feel liberated, free to develop more flexible values and to
admire others in a more genuine, less idealizing way" (p. 193). A
central part of this task of de-illusionment is reconciling oneself
with the dream—a challenge we will consider below.

The crisis of the limits represents a culmination of a developmental process begun at the very outset of adult life. The adolescent's sense of omnipotence—confidence about her or his future
and the impossibility of failure—effects high and very general
ideals. In the early years of adult living these ideals (meeting the
perfect lover; getting a job that will improve society) are tested
and necessarily delimited as they seek concrete expression. As family and career develop, further compromises and adjustments are
introduced. In the transition of the early forties an adult is invited
to re-examine the important ideals of youth—perhaps to acknowledge how little one has been able to do; perhaps to return to an
ideal abandoned in the busy accomplishment of adult life. The
maturing process at work here is a delimiting of ideals. Ideals necessarily general in youth have since been concretized in specific
choices of love and work. The limitations of these choices must

now be confronted, to be accepted as representative of personal limits or rejected in significant life changes that one now undertakes.

RECONCILING THE DREAM

In the increased interiority of the early forties, a person may return to the dream of young adulthood. The challenge in this recollection is to reconcile oneself with this dream (Levinson, pp. 245–50). Three different modes of reconciliation may occur.

One response is reckoning with the distance between the dream and one's achievement of it. Part of Levinson's de-illusionment phase, this reckoning need not be an experience of failure: I do not abandon my dream but modify and personalize it to better represent my aspirations at this point in life. The result of this reconciliation can be an increase in self-knowledge and self-acceptance and a mature focusing of my energies for the coming decades.

A second style of reconciliation is related to another characteristic of the dream—its potential tyranny. The adolescent dream is necessarily idealistic and accentuates only one aspect of the person. When relentlessly pursued, such a dream exercises a kind of tyranny. Other aspects of the individual atrophy; a single purpose controls life. When such a person is a married man, this tyranny will likely absorb his wife and her own dream as well. By the early forties such single-minded pursuit may well have produced much achievement, but the person may experience it as a hollow victory. This dream, achieved at too great a price, must now be re-evaluated—its tyranny identified and its force moderated to allow for more satisfying personal growth. This mode of reconciliation entails a letting go of the tyrannical part of the dream and a reintegration of the person with other, neglected parts of the self. It will also likely involve a rediscovery of spouse, family, and friends.

A third style of reconciliation involves a recovery of a dream that has been ignored. This is required when one realizes, in the reflectiveness which signals and induces the mid-life transition, that one's career choice in the twenties and its pursuit through the thirties has occurred at the expense of a deeper ambition or dream. I must now settle accounts with the dream betrayed, as I recognize, in Levinson's imagery, that I have climbed the wrong ladder. The urgency of this realization in the early forties arises from the conviction that this is the last chance one has to change. The dream, long ignored and only now reappearing, must be pursued *now* or it will be lost utterly. In such a recognition a person may undertake radical personal change, letting go a former career or lifestyle and "beginning again."

This mode of reconciliation is the experience today of many women in the mid-life transition. Culturally in the past a wife has been expected to play a supportive role in her husband's dream. The woman's own dream may well be lost in this process. Only in her early forties, with the children grown and leaving home, does a long-neglected dream make its shaky reappearance. Likewise a woman in a career may recognize at this time that she has performed according to others' expectations of the "appropriate" level of responsibility or creativity (for women) but not according to her own dream. Reconciliation with the dream in both instances may mean not only fostering the reawakened dream and deciding about a "second career" but also confronting and healing the anger and hostility that may accompany such a resurrected dream.

The turmoil that can surround these three styles of reconciliation recalls the importance of loved ones and a supportive community to assist an adult through this transition.

BALANCING THE POLARITIES

The Jungian orientation of Levinson's interpretation of the mid-life transition is displayed not only in his attention to an adult's dream but in his concentration on the process of individuation (pp. 209 ff.).[4] Levinson elaborates this mid-life process in terms of four polarities in the personality: the shifting balance of young and old, creative and destructive, masculine and feminine, and attachment and separateness. The rebalancing of these polarities at mid-life contributes to the adult's growth into mature generativity and to the release of those strengths which allow the person to become a caring and nonmanipulative mentor.

4. Levinson summarizes Jung: "Individuation is a developmental process through which a person becomes more uniquely individual. Acquiring a clearer and fuller identity of his own, he becomes better able to utilize his inner resources and pursue his own aims. . . . Jung was the first to recognize that individuation occurs, and is sorely needed, at mid-life and beyond" (p. 33). See also Jung (1964).

During this period of reflectiveness persons may become more acutely aware of age. The shift in time perspective, which we have mentioned before, helps to trigger thoughts of being "too old" for certain activities or styles. The humorous resistance to admitting one's age after thirty-nine thinly disguises this anxiety about no longer being young. Immature behavior during this period, a flight into a second adolescence, may signal an effort to recover some of the liveliness the individual sacrificed in the busy achievement of the previous decades. In the early forties adults are invited to rebalance the young and the old in themselves, letting go of aspects of their youthfulness now no longer appropriate and locating the values of maturity and experience in a new sense of the middle-aged self. A successful reintegration of this polarity releases the strengths appropriate to one's age and is remote preparation for the transition, still decades away, into old age.

The second polarity to come under review during this period is that of destructiveness and creativeness. Again, external events often set off this examination: The death or illness of a parent may raise questions of unresolved anger,[5] or the sheer accumulation of one's experience of the tragic and the absurd in life may bring deep hostilities to the surface. Personal aggressiveness, which has been channeled into a busy career or set aside in one's nurturance of a family, may now come under special scrutiny. Anger at parents or guilt over past destructiveness may reach a new level of awareness and demand healing. There is a need actively to forgive past wrongs and to come to terms with the destructiveness within and without the self. Such a reconciliation will also invite a person to make choices for the coming years that will reorder personal energies in more creative directions.

The balance of masculine and feminine in the personality, consolidated in late adolescence and early adulthood in response to cultural expectations of being a man or a woman, may come under review in the early forties. Several decades' experience of oneself—in both strengths and limitations—contributes to the

5. Vaillant found many of his subjects to be reworking their relationships with their parents during their mid-forties. Becoming aware of one's animosity toward parents was a prerequisite for subsequent reconciliation. Vaillant summarizes the struggle of one man in his late forties: "Once Sawyer was able to identify with his mother's aggressiveness rather than to be a passive victim of it, his life was changed" (p. 191).

need for this re-evaluation and to the confidence necessary to undertake it. At this time, for example, aspects of a man's personality that are judged as "feminine" (e.g., demonstrating gentleness or fear), and have therefore remained underdeveloped, may reappear and be welcomed into his behavioral style. For a woman, a sense of assertiveness which previously seemed to her "unwomanly" may find its way into her personality. The increased interiority of this period offers the opportunity to reflect on one's experience of being a woman or a man, allowing one to go beyond cultural stereotypes and expectations. The rebalancing of the polarity of masculine and feminine is especially important for the development of the person who would serve as a generative mentor for others. As we will discuss below, mentors function best when comfortable with their own sexuality and when able to illustrate an integrated attitude toward work and play, career and friendship. Such comfort results in part from a reworking of this important polarity within the maturing adult.

The fourth polarity, that of attachment and separateness (Levinson, p. 239), is most directly related to increased interiority. For Levinson, attachment means engagement in one's external environment. Growth in young adulthood involves the initiation of such engagement in career and intimate relationships. In the first decades of adult life family, community, and institutions play a vital and central role. In the mid-life transition an adult may feel drawn inward, toward the pole of separateness. By "separateness" Levinson refers to one's inner world—the life of the imagination, play, and reflection. The rebalancing of this polarity may entail a more powerful inclusion of the childlike strengths of imagination and play in the adult's personality and lifestyle. Refusal to question a busy attachment to job and external activities during this period will prevent a growth in interiority and this new awareness of one's own uniqueness and separateness. Working at a rebalancing of this polarity clears space to attend anew to the dream and to come to a new reconciliation with one's deepest and most personal ambitions and strengths.

The rebalancing of these polarities and the reconciliation of the dream lead to a new maturity, a maturity resulting from increased awareness and greater comfort with oneself. This maturity is also a development of generativity since it leads to a broader concern and a new kind of leadership.

GENERATIVE LEADERSHIP

Vaillant describes this movement toward leadership: "Almost always, full leadership involves a shift in career focus. Instead of delving progressively deeper into their specialized careers and acquiring progressively more competence, in middle life the men's career patterns suddenly diverged and broadened; they assumed tasks that they had not been trained for. Being truly responsible for others is no job for the specialist" (p. 227). A participant in Vaillant's study summarizes this shift in his own development: "The concerns that I have are now much less self-centered. From 30 to 40 they had to do with too many demands on too little money; whether I could make it in my profession; whether I was doing the best for my family, education for the children; etc. Post age 45 my concerns are more philosophical, more long term, less personal, and with a less intense feeling that all problems must be solved at once in my time. I *am* concerned about the state of human relations, and, especially of our society. I am concerned to teach others as much as I can of what I have learned" (p. 232).

This broadening of concern, complemented by a lessening of focus on one's own accomplishment, prepares a person to become a truly generative mentor. In the late thirties an adult often takes leave of his or her mentors (Levinson, p. 147). This change heralds both entry into greater independence and preparation for becoming a mentor oneself. An effective mentor is one who can care for the younger person without needing to manipulate. Generative care is here matched by detachment. Having come to terms with the need for power and achievement, the mentor can care altruistically for the other. This care for the other's development is complemented by the bittersweet realization that the younger person's growth will soon lead the other beyond the mentor's influence and care; thus as the mentor cares he or she prepares to let go.

The rebalancing of the polarity of masculine and feminine plays an especially important role in the development of the mature mentor. Having grown beyond either an accentuated masculinity or femininity and having overcome rigid distinctions between work and play, between career and friendship, the mentor is able to be both competent and tender. One might argue that this specific aspect of generative growth is a development toward androgyny: The person is now comfortable with complementary aspects of the self and this comfort provides a new kind of leadership in the community. If a generative mentor becomes, in this sense, androgynous, it is a growth that also arises from and depends on a clear sense of one's sexuality, tested and established through the twenties and thirties. Thus the mentor, as neither father nor mother, offers a quite different image of adult leadership. The generative leader is able to combine, perhaps for the first time, solicitude with detachment. Able to trust in the process of life and in the potential of the next generation, the generative person can let go the control and, even, manipulation which accompanied care in former years. Such care is generative as it begins to share with the next generation the control of the present and the design of the future.

This peculiar combination of care and detachment results in a self-transcendence which is characteristic of mature generativity. "What one has generated must be 'brought up,' guarded, preserved," notes Erikson, but it must ultimately be released and even "eventually transcended" (IR, p. 131). Through the psychological resources developed in the course of the mid-years I can now allow and even encourage new life to go its own way, even beyond my own control and influence. Generative care is able to let go, to release without bitterness, that which has been generated. But this mature letting go applies not only to the children and other works of our hands but to our very sense of self generated over the previous decades. Persons are more than what they do, more than the sum of what they have done. For many adults this is at best a fleeting insight. For many it is obscured over the busy years of early and middle adult life when so much energy is spent, appropriately, in the accomplishments which in turn tend to define persons, for themselves as well as for others. The development of mature generativity, as it involves altruism and detachment from more self-centered concern, entails a detachment from the strengths and limitations of our own accomplishments. This means neither a repudiation of what we have generated nor a move toward self-sufficiency apart from our generativity. This ultimate challenge of generativity does involve a letting go of what has been generated and an acceptance of ourselves apart from these accomplishments. This combination of a continued care and an increasing detachment prepares us for the invitations and demands of late adulthood.

SIX

Religious Generativity

Jesus is, for the Christian, a model of religious adulthood. At the start of our consideration of the religious dimensions of generativity let us dwell for a few moments on Jesus. To begin, let arise within you your own sense of Jesus as an adult. Note the images that come to you—from Scripture, from the liturgy, from prayer. Take some time to allow the images to arise.

Select one of these images that is particularly striking for you now, one that seems best to express your own sense of Jesus as a mature adult. Stay with the image for a while. Let it become full and concrete in detail.

As your image becomes rich in your awareness, these questions may enhance the reflection.

What does this image of Jesus say to you about the experience of personal power?

What does this image say to you about the awareness of oneself in adulthood?

What does this image of Jesus say to you about the experience and expression of mature care?

GENERATIVITY:
LEADERSHIP AND SERVICE

Religious generativity is the virtue by which mature Christians care for and shape their community. The religious challenge of generativity addresses the believer's work and creativity. Informed by the vision of Christianity, the generative adult contributes to the building up of the loving and just community, while handing on the faith to the next generation.

Christian generativity necessarily takes as its model the paradoxical life of Jesus Christ. A man who died in mid-adulthood and who fathered no children, Jesus is for the believer the essentially generative adult. His generativity is displayed not only in uncommon leadership[1] and an intense concern for his country and its future, but in the enduring religious tradition generated by his faith and action.

One of the most poignant expressions of Jesus' generative care is his concern for the future of Jerusalem: "How often would I have gathered your children together as a hen gathers her brood under her wings, and you would not!" (Matt. 23:37, Luke 13:34). Jesus' frustration, anger, and sharp sense of limitation give this text its special force. Preparing to let go both his own life and his previous hopes for Jerusalem, Jesus combines an intense concern with a trust in something greater than himself. This peculiar and difficult combination of care and detachment, formed by faith in God's presence in the world, describes Christian generativity. We will examine religious generativity here in its relationship to Christian ministry, to stewardship, and to reconciliation.

1. The sixth chapter of Mark's Gospel portrays powerfully this leadership of Jesus—his personal witness, preaching, and the mentoring of disciples—exercised in a cycle of intense social action and withdrawal for quiet and prayer.

DIAKONIA AND
CHRISTIAN MINISTRY

Religious generativity is expressed most centrally, perhaps, in service to the communities in which one lives. *Diakonia* is the New Testament term for such adult service or ministry.[2] *Diakonia,* as the action of believing adults, is action for others, action expressive of one's individual talents and gifts, and action in accord with the vision or dream of Christianity. It is the action of generative care expressed in teaching, in healing, in celebration—whatever the needs of the community. Such generative activity is also self-expression, since it matches the strengths of the individual to the needs of the community. This theology of ministry is grounded in Paul's understanding of the community as composed of adults with a variety of gifts, whose mutual care results both in individual growth and in the development of the community of faith (1 Cor. 12).

The actions of Christian service must be in accord with the community's vision. For Christians this is the dream of a healed world, a just and caring society. The realization of this dream, which Christianity inherited from Israel and has expressed in the imagery of the Kingdom, is to be both strenuously sought after and patiently awaited. As an expression of religious generativity, the action of the adult Christian must be in touch with the larger dream of the tradition. What is the relation between this larger vision and the individual's dream? How does a personal dream take energy and direction from this broader vision and yet remain true to its own uniqueness? Two near contemporaries, Ignatius Loyola and Martin Luther, witness to this creative merging of personal dream and Christian vision. Ignatius's dream contributed an influential new form of religious life and service that continues to this day in the Jesuits. Luther foresaw believers in a more intimate relationship with Scripture: The translation of the Bible into the vernacular was a gift of his religious generativity. Each of these personal visions was contested at the time of its emergence, yet

2. The noun "ministry," *diakonia,* appears in the Gospels only once (Luke 10:40). The verb *diakonein,* "to serve," and the related noun *diakonos,* "minister," appear throughout the New Testament. See especially John 12:26 on Christian servanthood.

each has contributed powerfully to the shape of modern Christianity.

If *diakonia* is the generative service that each believer is called to contribute to the community of faith, then ministry appears to be a requisite of Christian adulthood. All Christians are called to assume responsibility for the use of their gifts in the service of the Kingdom. A problem arises when the structure and understanding of ministry in a faith community do not allow for the generative participation of most of its adult members. When no access to religious leadership is provided for maturing adults, their religious maturation can be stunted—and this by the Church! It is a narrow interpretation of ministry which locates religious leadership in a small, specialized group. This discrimination within the community between a few select leaders and many followers is founded, in part, in a particular interpretation of religious childhood and maturity.

Adults remain, throughout the course of their lives, children of God. "Children" here captures, properly, the awareness of *belonging* as offspring and heirs and the recognition, by those who live in grace, of their insufficiency in their own salvation. While rejoicing in their status as children of God, however, adults do not fare as well as children of the clergy. This dependency, more acceptable in an era of educated clergy and generally uneducated laity, is experienced today as a hazard not only to psychological development but to religious growth. The risk is less in young adulthood: Many religious persons attest to the benefit to their own development of a religious mentor who served them, by approximation, as a kind of "father." Extrapolating from Vaillant and Levinson, however, we would argue that after forty it may be healthiest "to call no one father."[3]

A parallel and no less influential religious image is that of pastor or shepherd. This metaphor of care and commitment described the Lord in the Old Testament (Ps. 23, Is. 40:11) and Jesus in the Gospel of John (10:1–29). When this image of pastor is transferred to a minister or priest as Christ's representative, the

3. The Protestant insistence on the term "minister" rather than "priest" or "father" is germane here. Rejecting the authoritarian and hierarchical connotations of these latter terms, the early Reformers selected one that was rooted in New Testament usage and that conveyed more the orientation of service to the community.

metaphor is less apt. The symbol of pastor implies a radical distinction between guide and flock. This distinction not only contributes to an unfortunate isolation of clergy from laity but deprives the laity of their proper maturity as generative adults.[4]

Requisite for growth into religious generativity is a collegial model of ministry in the faith community. The hierarchical model, which has long dominated the practice if not the rhetoric of most denominations, sets the leader off from the community. He (and formal religious leadership in this model remains almost exclusively male) is seen as a sacred person, more a representative of God than a representative of the community's faith. A collegial model, on the other hand, understands the community as composed of a variety of ministers. These ministers, of differing expertise and training, serve each other in what can be called a "lateral ministry" (Egan, 1978). Such service, necessarily plural in form, allows many adults access to religious leadership and generativity. This *diakonia*, both collegial and lateral, is more likely to be a servant leadership (Greenleaf, 1977). In a structure of ministry guided by this model, the "professional" would not serve in isolation or solely in roles of dominance. Those leaders officially representing the Church would function among and along with a variety of generative adults, co-ordinating their service rather than replacing it.

FROM DISCIPLESHIP TO STEWARDSHIP

If all are called to exercise their talents in service to the community, adults are called to different modes of ministry at different times in life. The initial stage of adult life is characterized by much energy and by high ideals. Religiously this period can be described as one of discipleship.[5] During the twenties the young

4. In an address to the National Association of Priests' Councils in 1976 historian David O'Brien suggested that a better metaphor for this clergy-laity relationship would be that of sheep dog and sheep. Here both are of the same order of reality; the dog directs the flock with much clamor and energy but without significantly greater insight concerning the journey or its ultimate destination.

5. Much of the four Gospels is concerned with Jesus' selection and development of his disciples. Our colleague at the University of Notre Dame David

Christian responds to a call to serve, but often as a "follower." The believing community best responds to this stage of religious growth by structuring opportunities for young adults to test out their resources and their dreams of generous service. Opportunities for energetic and short-term service take advantage both of the idealism of this period and its provisional and exploratory character. Out of such vocational exploration some young adults will choose to pursue their religious dream in professional ministry in the Church.

Young adulthood is a time of apprenticeship; the disciple is the religious equivalent of the apprentice. A beginner in religious productivity, the disciple is a follower and in need of a religious mentor. For the Christian, Jesus functions as the mentor par excellence, encouraging his disciples to follow him and to exercise themselves in service to others. Christ likewise displayed the challenging combination of care for the disciples and the ability to let go of his direction of them. When the dynamic of mentoring is not accompanied by a capacity to let go, so that one's disciples can themselves become stewards and mentors for others, the generative process is frustrated. Jesus' death, premature and traumatic as it was, terminated this first stage of his mentoring[6] and provided the space for the apostles and disciples to move into fuller leadership and stewardship in the fledgling Church. Christ's letting go of his leadership role and his turning over this stewardship to the next generation, signaled in his giving of the keys to Peter, is powerfully portrayed in his final discourse to the disciples in John's Gospel. A new mutuality has developed: "No longer do I call you servants . . . but I have called you friends" (15:15). Earlier in the discourse he encourages their religious generativity: "He who believes in me will also do the works that I do; and *greater works* than these he will do . . ." (14:12; our emphasis).

The transition for the adult Christian from discipleship to stewardship is a necessary step in religious development. Stew-

Burrell suggests that Luke's Gospel charts a movement from discipleship (generally chaps. 4–11) to stewardship (chaps. 16–19).

6. Jesus' relationship to believers after his death and resurrection was a mentoring of a different kind, one that was increasingly received through ecclesial interpretations of Christ. Schweizer discusses this transition in *Lordship and Discipleship* (1960, pp. 77 ff.).

ardship[7] represents mature leadership; one's service and energies are now focused on that "broader concern" which characterizes full generativity. A steward is one who cares for the household and who administers the larger community. This expression of religious generativity is concerned with handing on the faith and is often exercised by becoming a mentor. Such mature leadership and care may begin for some in their thirties but can be expected by the forties, when an adult's growth in self-awareness and self-acceptance allows him or her to care for young adults in noncontrolling and nonmanipulative ways.

The challenge to the Christian community is, as we have already noted, to provide both the expectation and the structure for such a transition to generative leadership in its adults. If religious leadership is restricted to a small group of persons, whether priests or other professionals, the community will be deprived of a healthy variety of ministers. By blocking this development and expansion of ministry, the Church imperils the handing on of the faith.

RELIGIOUS DIMENSIONS OF THE MID-LIFE PASSAGE

The mid-life transition experienced by many in their early forties can be interpreted as a religious passage. A passage, as we saw in Chapter Two, describes a potentially dangerous shift from one state in life to another. My former state and its values and motives are no longer satisfying; they no longer make sense. Disorientation and confusion can result. Such a passage is, for one who would believe, a potentially sacred time, a *kairos*. Experienced initially as disorienting and even debilitating, this time is also one of special opportunity—an extraordinary chance to encounter God and to reorient oneself in more loving and generous directions. This *kairos* at mid-life, like every other such frightening moment, is often avoided. Busying oneself in work or fleeing into distracting and even promiscuous activity are but two such attempts.

---

7. The steward (*oikonomos*) in the New Testament is one who administers the community. This co-ordinating of the affairs of the community is a leadership role; it is also a servant's role, since one works for the Lord. See Luke 16–19 on stewardship; Matt. 25 on servants who are entrusted with important work in their master's absence; 1 Cor. 4 on religious stewardship.

One's community and loved ones become crucial contributors to an individual's recognition and resolution of this passage. A religious community's role is not to distract a person until the crisis is over, but actively to assist the person to confront its perilous challenges so that, within the psychological stress of this time, God's unanticipated but inviting presence can be discerned. Here we shall examine the religious dimensions of the mid-life passage and the religious community's ministry within it.

The passage in mid-life has special characteristics. First, it is more related to age than to one's level of achievement. The changes in life-satisfaction and personal motivation that occur at this time appear to be independent of one's level of success. The loss of a job may trigger this crisis for one person; a promotion will instigate similar self-examination for another (Levinson, 1978, p. 301). Second, this transition in the mid-years is experienced as an embarrassment. Expecting and expected to be mature, to be "stable," the middle-aged adult is embarrassed to be caught in such personal upheaval. From a religious perspective the tragedy of this embarrassment is that it often leads to an attempt to disguise the passage, from oneself as well as from others. A person tries to pretend that nothing has really changed, that his life is still under control. A disguised passage is doubly perilous: I do not confront it myself, and it remains hidden from those others who might care for me. Others cannot assist me in the negotiation of an adult passage if they (and I) are unaware of its occurrence.

The increased interiority of the mid-years, as we have noted, invites the busy adult to explore the mode and extent of her generative participation in life. This interiority may instigate a new interest in things of the spirit, calling for a reconciliation with the dream and a rebalancing of the significant polarities in one's life. For the religious person this personal dream or ambition will likely be related to the sense of vocation—the ideal that I feel called to live out in my life of love and work. One of the tasks of this mid-life passage, then, will be to re-examine the dream-as-vocation. This re-examination may entail "de-illusionment," a coming to terms with the practical limitations of my ability to live out my high ideals. It may demand freeing myself from the tyrannical control of a dream that is really someone else's. It may entail recovery and reinvestment in a dream long neglected. Deeper confirmation in my vocation, as well as a decision for change, may result from this mid-life re-examination.

There are also religious dimensions to the rebalancing of polarities that Levinson noted as characteristic of the mid-years. Confrontation in middle life with the polarities of young and old in myself may give me deliverance from the culture's glorification of youth. At last I become free to relish the advantages, the graces, of *this* age in my life. I may also recapture those strengths of religious childlikeness which I had lost in my energetic entry into the more calculated and controlled world of adult responsibilities. Letting go the inappropriate illusions of youth and the fears of growing old, the middle-aged person can become more open to the present, more aware of the presence of self and of God.

The reordering of the polarity of destructive and creative impulses finds religious resonance in the need to forgive and to be forgiven. The interiority of this time often resurrects grievances of the past—guilt over my own destructive patterns and condemnation of others for their destructiveness in my life. In such a time of regret and recrimination the religious intuition offers hope for healing, and the religious community witnesses to the possibility of forgiveness. Recollection of the pain and injuries of the past can produce confusion and anger; it can also provide a unique opportunity for reconciliation. The healing of the destructiveness in my own life integrates and reorganizes personal energies in more creative directions.

The heightened experience of interiority in mid-life contributes in a special way to the reworking of the polarities of attachment and separateness. In Levinson's use (p. 239), the term separateness signifies neither isolation nor estrangement; rather it reflects involvement in one's inner world. This is the world of imagination and play; it is also the domain of prayer. For a believer, increased attention to his inner life, its values and motives, leads to prayer and meditative reflection. Thus the introspection of the mid-years can lead to a greater comfort in being alone and an increased detachment from the external norms of achievement. This religious reintegration does not necessarily demand a retreat from engagement in society, but it often requires some change in the quality of this engagement. More comfortable now with solitude, more in touch with my own motives and limitations, I feel that my interaction with the world will exhibit both a more personal and a more altruistic quality.

In the rebalancing of the masculine and feminine aspects of personality in middle age there is an opportunity for moving beyond exaggerated notions of male and female. The religious tradition can assist or thwart this personal reassessment of one's sexual identification and role. Thus, one strand within Christianity argues from Jesus' masculinity to the restriction of priestly leadership roles to men (Seper, 1977). Yet another understanding of Jesus finds him less univocally "male" and more the embodiment of an androgynous ideal of an adult who is both competent and tender, who combines assertiveness with vulnerability. The rebalancing of the polarities of these sexual stereotypes will strengthen one's development as a religious mentor, an adult who is comfortable with one's own "feminine" and "masculine" inclinations and thus available as a genuine friend and colleague to both men and women. When a community includes a range of such mature and generative adults, the next generation is well served. These mature persons—priests and lay persons, women and men who do not need to control in order to contribute—exhibit an androgynous style of leadership, one that is at once caring and effective. In its richest moments, such a community signals that future where there is "neither male nor female" (Gal. 3:28).

RITES OF RECONCILIATION AT MID-LIFE

Often the effort to avoid or to disguise the mid-life passage is related to its unexpectedness; the result may be that the transition is experienced unreflectively and alone. But, as we have seen, research indicates that this passage is a patterned occurrence, an often disconcerting but prevalent psychological event to be expected in one's middle adult years. The normal pattern and expectable sequence here suggest the necessity of rites of passage to support the successful transition into mature middle age. The development of these rites would assist in the recognition, exploration, and celebration of this mid-years passage, in which reconciliation is a major theme.

It may be useful to mention here for clarification our earlier distinction between rites and ritual. We use "rites" to refer to the wide variety of ways in which a community responds to the dangers and opportunities of a critical transition. These include activities of counseling, of education, of support and celebration. "Ritual" designates the specific, often liturgical, exercises or "religious services" by which a believing community focuses on some important aspect of a passage. In this sense a liturgical ritual is one of the rites that surround and assist a passage. In recent Catholic usage the "rite of reconciliation" refers to the sacramental ritual of penance or confession. Our broader use of the phrase here recalls the variety of ways, some quite informal and unofficial, in which we experience reconciliation with one another and with God. These less formal religious reconciliations do not replace the sacramental event, but can complement and enliven this traditional form of religious healing.

The rites of passage at mid-life, then, would first assist in the recognition of the passage, rescuing the experience from its hidden or disguised manifestations. Adult education and support groups in a parish, for instance, can help persons realize that they are not alone in the experience of mid-life confusion. Embarrassment, which often serves to isolate, can be overcome in the realization that the disorientation of this period is expectable, even developmentally sound. Such "educational rites" help to schedule the crisis, enabling adults to anticipate and even prepare for its occurrence.

Second, rites of the mid-life passage would provide opportunity for exploration, inviting the person to confront the developmental tasks of this time. Growth groups with capable leaders, for example, can provide the caring and protective atmosphere in which an adult attempts to reconcile her dream and to balance anew the polarities and ambiguities within the self. Programs of leadership development can assist maturing Christians to focus their generative energies more broadly in activities of social concern and ministry. Such explicit attention to the details and dynamic of these transitions can support adults in identifying and responding to the graces, limitations, and failures that have shaped their lives. In such heightened awareness the processes of forgiveness, healing, and reorientation can begin.

Those who would attend or minister to this transition must themselves possess maturity and skills. The questions and fears which arise at this time often lead religious persons to seek the

mission statement

counsel of a ministering person. It is the minister's personal maturity rather than status or ecclesiastical office that will ground an effective ministry to this mid-life passage. Thus the minister must have dealt maturely with his or her own dream, recognizing its illusions and tyranny, accepting its continuing invitations for renewal and change. In addition to personal maturity, the minister should acquire a working understanding of the developmental crises of adult life and of their religious possibilities. Finally the minister should develop those skills which encourage and challenge others to honest self-assessment and self-acceptance. With such awareness and skill, the minister can then invite others to experience the reconciliations of this time as spiritual exercises of Christian adulthood.

With the support of loved ones and, often, the assistance of a skilled minister, an adult in middle age can come to a renewed sense of self and of her generative engagement in the world. Now a third aspect of these rites of passage comes into view—celebration of the transition into a new stage of life. The middle phase of the passage is, as we have noted, pre-eminently exploratory and educational; this concluding phase is liturgical and communal. With this celebration a person is welcomed not back to a former state in life from which one had fallen but into a new stage in life. Forgiveness of the past and reconciliation with the dream have released new energies and hope. These are to be celebrated as the community gives thanks for the good that God has accomplished in its midst. The celebration is for the community as well as for the individual in passage. Its action announces that this crucial transition exists, that the believer can hope to find God within it and can, thus, expect successful resolution. This celebration invites others in the community to self-examination and to preparation for similar meetings with God in their own adult lives.

The culmination of these rites of passage, in a ritual action in which the person is incorporated again into the community, can be understood religiously as an event of reconciliation. Reconciliation is a category of Christian growth elaborated in St. Paul's letters to the Corinthians and the Romans: "All this is from God, who through Christ reconciled us to himself and gave us the ministry of reconciliation; that is, in Christ God was reconciling the world to himself, not counting their trespasses against them, and entrusting to us the message of reconciliation" (2 Cor. 5:18–19).

"For if while we were enemies we were reconciled to God by the death of his Son, much more, now that we are reconciled, shall we be saved by his life" (Rom. 5:10). In these core statements[8] Paul describes a peacemaking between former enemies, a healing of the gap between the world and God, between body and spirit. He also locates this activity in God, both prior to our response and also the condition for our subsequent salvation. Of special interest here, however, is his reference to God's giving us "the ministry of reconciliation." What shape has this ministry taken?

If baptism represents the first and crucial reconciliation of God and the Christian, the believing community soon found it necessary to devise other ministries of reconciliation for erring believers.[9] Recognizing that baptism was too profound a conversion to be repeated, the early Church elaborated the rite of penance for those whose public infidelity demanded acknowledgment and formal reconciliation. The sacrament of penance was gradually extended, becoming part of the ministry to the dying, then a means for a more ordinary and frequent reconciliation with God. In a later development of Catholic piety, the sacrament became a devotional exercise with less direct relationship to a movement of crucial reorientation or conversion. The new rite of reconciliation in the Roman Catholic community attempts to recover both the communal dimensions of the reconciliation and its relationship to one's primary conversion in faith.[10]

Over the course of this elaboration a nondevelopmental understanding of reconciliation came to predominate. Reconciliation was interpreted as a *return* from sin to a former, lost state of purity. Here the dialectic is between sinfulness and a fixed ideal of perfection. An alternate, more developmental understanding of reconciliation is possible, one more appropriate to the rites of the mid-life passage.

The reconciliation demanded in mid-life is not a return to a for-

8. For other New Testament statements about reconciliation see Matt. 5:24, Acts 7:26, Rom. 11:15, 1 Cor. 7:11, Eph. 2:16, and Col. 1:20, 22.

9. For a brief history of this development see Paul Anciaux (1962). See also Monika Hellwig (1972, pp. 81 ff.) on the historical question of rebaptizing those who had been excluded from the Church.

10. See *The Rite of Penance* (1975), also Walter Burghardt's (1974) discussion of reconciliation in the light of concern for justice and ecological balance.

mer balance and maturity, from which I have fallen during this time of crisis or distress. It is a reconciliation within myself and of myself with God. Reckoning with the dream and reordering the polarities in my life are part of the task. I become reconciled with my past, acknowledging personal limitations and sinfulness in a way not possible before. This interior reconciliation (with myself and with God) must often be accompanied by reconciliation with loved ones—spouse, parents, children, friends. In the liturgical celebration of the mid-life passage, in the midst of the Eucharist or as a part of a communal experience of the sacramental rite of reconciliation, for example, this reconciliation is acknowledged and celebrated in the community of faith. The person, after some difficulty and struggle, has reached a new and grace-filled stage in life. The healing and reconciliation which have been experienced will release new energies in the person, which, in the shape of a broader care and a more altruistic concern for others, will benefit many in the believing community and beyond.

A suggestion arising from this reflection is that the Church explore the ministry of reconciliation in relation to specific developmental crises of growth in adult life. In the mid-life passage, in retirement, as well as in divorce and in a gay adult's maturation, there are special moments which call for forgiveness and reintegration of the past and which are also opportunities for exceptional growth. When the traditional sacrament of reconciliation is understood in relation to these specific challenges of adult religious growth, it will take on greater meaning and enjoy a renaissance in Catholic practice. Faith communities can minister to these difficult passages with a wide variety of rites of reconciliation—exercises in acknowledgment, education, support, and ritual that represent a contemporary form of the *"diakonia* of reconciliation" first remarked by Paul in his letter to the Corinthians.

SUCCESSFUL AND UNSUCCESSFUL PASSAGE

Although the need to re-evaluate one's life and its future direction is a patterned and expectable event in mid-life, an adult can choose not to respond to these urgings. This religious passage can be refused or aborted. When this occurs, the result is religious stagnation. An individual may have a growing sense of being unproductive, of "not going anywhere," and yet not know how to initiate change. A person may come to realize that his productivity does not extend much beyond himself; one may be creative—in children, in works—but these creations appear now as controlled extensions of the self. As proof of the person's self-worth, they cannot be let go, cannot be given away. Religiously, this represents a failure of self-transcendence and can result in self-absorption.

Most often the refusal to confront the mid-life passage is grounded in one of two responses to the challenges of mature generativity. The first response is fear. The adult may be distant from any personal dream or have little sense of creativity. Renegotiating the inner polarities is too threatening: I am already vaguely afraid of growing old, of the ambiguities of my continuing destructive urges, of being alone. To face these issues directly is simply too dangerous. The terror of the passage is rejected in favor of an apparently "safer" future. The coming years are approached as a time of holding on rather than of giving oneself away. Manifested, perhaps, in decreasing social involvement (staying at home more, watching more television) and other insulating behaviors, the person's life levels off. On such a plateau one is better able to protect against unexpected and unmanageable changes, to defend against further invitations to grow, whether these be from one's inner self, from other persons, or from God. Adult life thus becomes religiously stagnant.

A different response arises from a person with a more active and powerful sense of self. Such a person may fail to negotiate this passage through an inability to give up or to share control. Having become accustomed to the blend of care and control appropriate to the thirties, I may be unable in middle age to alter this combination and learn to care more altruistically; I cannot lessen control, whether in regard to my children or my job. Unable to let go, I lack the essential religious ability to "hand on" adult responsibility to the next generation. The acuteness of this inability may not be realized until the fifties, when younger people, whether grown children, students, or junior colleagues, are increasingly seen as threats to one's control and authority.

Handing on the tradition—an essentially generative act—involves a loss of control. As "traditioners," rather than reproducing the next generation in our image and thus repeating ourselves, we gradually turn over to the next generation our society, its institutions, and even Christian faith. The challenge of mature generativity is to trust in the generational process, for certainly the next generation will alter what we hand on to them. For the religious person this trust is in God's guiding presence within the community of faith. The Spirit is with us from generation to generation; no individual need function as sole controller and guarantor of this transition. An instance of religious generativity frustrated is the pastor who cannot share authority and cannot, in later years, let go his control. He not only deprives himself of the religious growth to be experienced in such trusting surrender; he likewise retards the development of the next generation of ministers. Like overgrown children, they must await the enforced "letting go" of his death to effect the handing on to them of the roles and responsibilities of religious leadership.

If religious stagnation describes a condition of being trapped in oneself, successful passage through the challenges of generativity is recognized in the release of new energies and the confidence to go beyond oneself in altruistic service. Reconciliation with one's dream means release from some of the illusions of earlier years and a consequent, more realistic, acceptance of oneself. ("I'm not going to accomplish as much as I had planned, but what I do is good.") A reworking of the inner polarities produces greater comfort with growing older and with aspects of the self (tenderness, assertiveness) that once seemed inappropriate. The person has also forgiven and tamed some of the destructive forces within and has found new resources in quiet and solitude. These shifts can make the generative person more available to others. Less driven by inner demands and social pressures, my energies become available to the community in a new way.

In the first chapter we observed that childlikeness appears in the New Testament as a paradoxical ideal of maturity. The graceful passage into generativity highlights personal traits that are suggestive of this childlikeness. A child is less defined by sexuality than is a young adult and is in touch with the destructive forces of personality (often in the guise of the demons and goblins of his or her imagination). The child can enjoy time alone, in play and in personal fantasy. In some ways, then, the fully generative person may begin to look like a child. The seriousness of one's career is less dominant; it is less necessary to "play for keeps." Browning

(1973) suggests that the generative person displays a new blending of work and play. In the maturity of middle age, play—the assimilation and shaping of reality—emerges as a significant complement to work, which more often represents an accommodation to reality.[11] Vaillant found the ability to incorporate play into one's adult lifestyle, in forms of sports and games and vacations, to be a clear indicator of mature adaptation. Play involves an ability to trust, both oneself and others.[12] This trust, required if we are to remain playful, is a common victim of the demands and pressures of becoming a "grownup." An abiding grace of the mid-life transition is its opportunity to recover some of these abandoned qualities of childlikeness. By delivering me from the earlier adult self-seriousness and its accompanying need for control, this passage prepares me for the playful maturity required to enter the Kingdom of God.

This new maturity also prepares a person to be a religious mentor. No longer so taken with his own goals for relationships, with less need to be defensive about his limitations, the generative person is able to attend more freely and altruistically to a younger person's growth. Greater trust in God's presence in life allows me to see younger colleagues not as threats to my authority and harbingers of my obsolescence but as companions with whom I can share control and responsibility. The transition into generativity for the religious person is a passage into stewardship. That resource of the community which demands the greatest attention and care is the next generation of believers. A challenge for the believing community is to be able to recognize and call forth those who have reached the maturity required for the mentoring and stewardship of this resource of faith.

Growth into mature religious generativity results in a new com-

11. The distinction of play as assimilation and work as accommodation that Browning uses is Piaget's. He sums up this new synthesis of work and play: "Rationality, for generative man, is associated with the total wisdom of the organism—the total adaptive task of conforming to the specifics of reality while at the same time forcing reality to conform obediently to man's need and propensities" (p. 190).

12. "It is hard to separate capacity to trust from capacity to play, for play is dangerous until we can trust both ourselves and our opponents to harness rage. In play, we must trust enough and love enough to risk losing without despair, to bear winning without guilt, and to laugh at error without mockery" (Vaillant, 1977, p. 309).

bination of virtues in the personality. Charity, matured into less controlling care and a broader concern, is now joined by detachment. Charity is manifested in ·the generative person's contribution to the community and society. In middle age this self-giving is informed by greater self-knowledge and less restricted by one's personal ambition and the need to succeed. Detachment is that peculiar virtue that allows one to let go of control. It is rooted not in a stoic indifference but in a conviction—perhaps new for the adult—that God rather than oneself will see to the destiny of future generations of believers and nonbelievers. The energetic self-investment in Christian service characteristic for many in the twenties and thirties may be transformed in the forties and fifties into a self-investment complemented by a new disengagement. Control can now be shared and passed on as one becomes able to trust more fully both in God and the next generation. This virtue of detachment does not manifest itself in a decrease in one's involvement or creativity but rather in a growth in trust, patience, and an ability to share responsibility. The religious insight which allows such mature generativity is that the human and Christian enterprise extends beyond my strengths and limitations. Thus I learn to give myself to something that transcends me. And in giving myself away, I find myself again, now in a new relationship with God and the community.

GENERATIVITY AND LEAVING AN "AFTERWARDS"

Mencius, the Confucian scholar of the third century before Christ, delivered an important observation on the human challenge of generativity. Speaking in the cultural context of China's concern for offspring and insistence upon the virtue of filial piety, Mencius declared, "There are three unfilial things, and the greatest of these is to have no posterity."[13] A literal translation of Mencius' Chinese gives us this intriguing phrase: ". . . the great one [of these] is having *no afterwards* [*wu hou*]." It can be said with safety that all Chinese who have read this sentence since Mencius have understood the phrase "no afterwards" to mean

13. We have altered slightly James Legge's translation in his *The Works of Mencius* (1970), p. 313.

"no posterity," having no children. And yet the words say more than this. The attractive ambiguity of this Chinese phrase suggests the human need and challenge to be generative—a generativity which, for most, begins in childbearing but includes all the ways we seek to contribute to life, to fashion something for the future, and to leave behind an "afterwards." "Afterwards" also highlights the dual aspect of human generativity: The word refers to the legacy that we attempt to assemble but also reminds us that things survive *after* us. We leave them behind as they escape our ultimate control. Here again we see the stark challenge of generativity: at some point to allow my productions (children, works) to be set free, to be appreciated as more than an extension of myself. Thus, as we have seen, within the psychological challenge and the virtue of generativity is the dual demand to engage myself and then to let go.

One of the important contributions of Christianity to human civilization has been its reminder that generativity is a more than physical and familial imperative. Christianity's rich tradition of celibacy has modeled adult generativity in lifestyles that are not grounded in the creation of children, but in which creativity and care are expressed in a broader concern for what has been generated.[14] Celibate Christians respond to the same need to be generative; they too must concern themselves with an "afterwards" and their own legacy. They experience the same temptations as physical parents to cling to and control their creations, and they feel the same call, in the most mature stage of generativity, to let go of these productions and entrust them to a future that they themselves will not see.

Generativity as a Christian virtue translates the self-giving of a celibate Christian in more positive terms than the traditional presentation of the celibate as a "eunuch for the sake of the Kingdom." More significant than a decision not to generate physical

14. Vaillant's comment on generativity among the unmarried is of note: "The church, the teaching professions, and perhaps the armed forces contain highly generative individuals . . . who have never married. In their twenties, many such men and women have experienced real difficulty with intimacy, yet over the years they have managed to give richly of themselves to the next generation and to grow in the process. I suspect it is not coincidence that such individuals all achieve strong group allegiance, as if the security of group membership provides them the security and strength that most adults find in one-to-one intimacy" (p. 216).

offspring is a person's creative concentration of personal energy on the future of the Church and human society. Mature celibates hope this future will bear something of their mark, but accept the invitation of generativity to give themselves away, believing in a fruitfulness that they will not experience. The Christian community stands today as the beneficiary of centuries of this devoted celibate generativity.

SEVEN

Development in Mature Age

REFLECTION

How do we learn about growing older and being old? From our culture, our families, our colleagues, our friends, . . . and, in due time, from personal experience as well. Consider your own experience. Where are older persons in your own world? Does your awareness of aging come from personal experience—do you think of yourself as old? Are there older persons among your close friends and family—those with whom you share your life in significant ways? Are the elderly among your colleagues or your clients—those with whom and for whom you work? Does your sense of the aged come from the culture and the media—from film or newspapers or television or advertising? Take some time to locate these sources of information in your own experience.

Now, consider what you have learned about aging from these sources. Select a person who is an example to you of someone who has grown old well.

What do you admire most about this person?

What do you learn from this person about the negative experiences of growing older and being old?

What do you learn from this person about the positive experiences of growing older and being old?

It is not easy to be old in America. Growing older seems an affront to one's self-image, a deterrent to one's plans, and a general inconvenience to society. The fact that aging is inevitable does little to soften its negative aspect. It seems rather to heighten our anxiety about our own aging and our guilt over the poor way in which we treat those among us who are old. And yet there are hints that this negative story of aging is not the full account. Most of us hope for a long life, even though we are ambiguous about being old. Literature and history recount stories of the richness of a long life well lived. Religious images in many traditions speak of a depth of spirit available only to the sage. The poet promises that "the best is yet to be."

Within the social sciences the emerging field of gerontology—the study of mature age and the processes of aging—suggests that through its final decades human life continues to be characterized by opportunities for development and personal growth. A significant contribution of gerontology has been to alert us to the diversity that exists among older persons. The unique events of each life history result over the life-span in a richly individualized personality. Adults differ among themselves in more ways, and in more significant ways, than do children. This diversity is not lessened in late adulthood. The tendency to group older Americans into a stereotyped category of "the aged," with supposedly similar experiences, expectations, and needs, is misleading. When this stereotype is largely negative and functions as an influence in the development of public policy, the consequences can be sinister both for the old and for the young—who know that they shall one day be old. "The aged" do not exist—only particular persons in a particular phase of their own life's experience. But negative stereotypes of growing older and being old prevail, among young and old alike.

Many older persons whose experience of their own life in their sixties and seventies is one of competence and satisfaction nevertheless retain negative images of "older people" in general (National Council on Aging, 1975). They judge their own circumstances to be a fortunate exception rather than evidence of newly emerging styles of aging. But as attention is paid to the accumulating experience of that majority of persons who grow old both gracefully and vigorously, we become more aware of the rich possibility of human life that remains throughout its course. Bernice Neugarten (1975), for example, speaks of the emergence of the "young-old," a lifestyle that predominates among Americans in their sixties and seventies and already contradicts many of the cultural images of aging. The young-old, as a group, are "markedly different from the outmoded stereotypes of old age. They are relatively free from traditional social responsibilities of work and family, they are relatively healthy, relatively well-off, and they are politically active" (p. 8). These qualities are likely to become more and more characteristic of older Americans in the decades ahead.

This is not to suggest that the current negative stereotype of aging should be replaced by equally naive utopian predictions. It is rather to alert us to both the possibilities and the diversities that exist in the mature years of adulthood.

THE CHALLENGE OF MATURE AGE

There are common tasks which confront every older person. As one ages, more attention has to be given to maintaining health and to compensating for declining physical vigor. The social world of the older person undergoes major shifts. Most older persons have some experience of retirement, either voluntary or enforced, and must adjust to the social and financial changes that retirement introduces. New roles are adopted (leisured senior citizen, widow, pastor emeritus), and former roles must be adapted in a flexible way (after retirement, how do I relate to my spouse? my former work colleagues? my adult children and their families?). There are questions of new living arrangements. Should we keep the house or get a smaller apartment? Should we move to a better climate or stay here where we have roots? In the death of my spouse or a lifelong friend, I am deprived of a person whose presence cannot be replaced easily in my old age. Now that I am alone, should I move to be closer to my married children or strike out on my own? Can I care for my own needs or will I have to move to a nursing home? One's satisfaction and adjustment in mature age will be influenced by the way in which these age-related tasks are accomplished. These developmental tasks also serve as the context for the emergence of inner resources that are particular to the mature personality (Havighurst, 1953 and 1961).

The social and personal changes of the mature years intensify the movement of interiority that begins for many in middle age. In the midst of these changes I ask the question "What does my life mean?" It is a question asked of the present. But with my present life in flux I look to my past and my future for cues and clues to my current significance. In old age there is the realization that there is not much time in my personal future. Most of my life is behind me. The possibility of my own death is real and immediate. If *now* is meaningless, there is not much time left to do something which will confer meaning on the present or make up for lack of meaning in the past. There is dynamic interplay between past and present meaning. As I look to the past to discern what my life means, I am likely to respond in a combination of acceptance and rejection. If I can say yes to the present, my present, I am likely to affirm the past which has brought me to today. If, however, today is an unpleasant reality, I may curse the past that has brought me to this plight. I may blame others or myself, but I blame rather than take responsibility. It is true that a remembrance of an affirming past can contribute to an acceptance, even an appreciation, of the present. But often one's memory and evaluation of the past are clouded by present negative feeling.

The challenge to come to a sense of the meaning of one's life involves a re-evaluation of both one's present and one's past. Part of the challenge of the mature years arises in the necessity to transcend the several sources of personal identity and significance that appropriately characterize middle adulthood. Through much of my adult life I have been identified by and have identified with the roles and responsibilities and products of my social involvement. I have been spouse, parent, worker, leader, citizen, householder. Gradually over the course of late adulthood these various roles are either removed (the role of worker is removed at retirement; the role of spouse is removed by the death of the other) or significantly changed (the role of parent is changed as both parent and adult child age). I must let go of some earlier responsibilities and renegotiate my involvement in others. To do this, I must be able to gamble precisely that sense of myself as a competent, generative, and involved adult that signaled my successful resolution of the challenge of middle adulthood. I must risk having these essential personality strengths of my middle age altered as I move into maturity. I must be open to the possibility of a new sense of myself and of the significance of my life.

This movement into a new stage of personality expansion in late adulthood depends upon the strengths of one's generative middle age. It is only in the person who "in some way has taken care of things and people and who has adapted . . . to the triumphs and disappointments of being the originator of others or the generator of products and ideas" (CS, p. 268) that the full fruits of human maturity may ripen. The challenge of human maturity in old age requires the strengths that are developed in generativity. I need the capacity for commitment, responsibility, and nurturance that are developed by "taking care of things and people." I need the self-confidence, the flexibility and tolerance, and especially the sense of humor that are developed as I adapt "to the triumphs and disappointments of being an originator"—whether through parenthood or in other forms of creative involvement in a world that goes beyond myself. These resources of the generative adult are required for the movement into full human maturity. But in this movement they are transformed and transcended. In the psychological challenge of mature age my characteristic ability to care for others is tested as the demands for disinterested concern become an invitation to responsible renunciation.

As the question of meaning comes to prominence in the mature years, it arouses a range of responses—impulses that have been present before but only in rudiment. Impulses toward self-acceptance, integrity, and wholeness struggle against a pervading sense of despair and disgust. Each of these is a possible response to the ambiguous evidence of one's own life. Each is a possible judgment on my life and, through my life, on the human enterprise. Out of the conflict engendered by these opposing impulses there can emerge new strengths of the personality that were only potentially available before.

The psychological challenge of mature age, then, focuses upon the individual's evaluation of his or her life as meaningful or absurd. The challenge is favorably resolved when the impulses for wholeness and affirmation outweigh the impulses for negation and despair. I move toward a basic appreciation of my life as having been inevitable, appropriate, and meaningful. The strain between affirmation and despair in my life is not dissolved. It remains a dynamic tension, but one in which meaning prevails.

INTEGRITY: THE STRENGTH OF MATURE AGE

Erikson calls this mature stage, the full fruit of human development, integrity. Understood as a resource of the mature personality, integrity is seen in "the acceptance of one's one and only life cycle and of the people who have become significant to it as something that had to be and that, by necessity, permitted no substitutions" (IYC, p. 139). I am able to look at life in terms of my own life, its particularities and peculiarities, the patterns it shares with the lives of others, and its idiosyncrasies, with the judgment that it could not have been otherwise. This judgment is made not in despair ("No wonder I turned out so poorly, given all that I have suffered") nor in pride ("See how well my life has gone"). It is rather an affirmation of the "givenness"—the inevitability—of my own life's course. This sense of inevitability comes in retrospect. It is rooted in an acceptance of the goodness of *now*. Because I accept myself and my meaning now, I can look back to salute the drama of pain and joy that has brought me to this point. The expected and unexpected happenings of my life are all vitally related to who I am now. Therefore I can accept them as they were; I can affirm that it is good that my life has gone as it has. If events had been different along the way, I would have become someone different. These differences might have made my life "better," according to some criteria. But I would not be who I am.

This self-acceptance brings both freedom from my past and a deeper respect for its power in my life even to the present. And it can bring as well "a new and different love of one's parents, free of the wish that they should have been different, and an acceptance of the fact that one's life is one's own responsibility" (IYC, p. 139). Parents are one of the crucial inevitabilities of life. Much of psychological growth throughout life is involved in dealing with one's parents—identifying with them in childhood, rejecting them in adolescence, identifying oneself apart from them in early adulthood. In this process parents can become scapegoats. "If only my parents had been different. . . ." It is true that if my parents had been different, I would be different. It may be true that my parents have been in good part responsible for difficulties of maturity or personality that assail me now. But it is not until I can move beyond blaming "them" that I can start to take adult responsibility for myself.

This movement begins in forgiveness, an acceptance of my parents for what they are and an acceptance of what I have become under their influence. This forgiveness frees me to take responsibility for what I wish to become on my own. As I am able to free myself from my own ambivalent dependence on my parents, I am able to move toward a more mature love of them—in themselves and for their part in my life. Through the mid-years, aspects of my parents are reassimilated into an adult sense of self. In mature age this acceptance of self can deepen into a profound appreciation for all those persons—parents and others—who have influenced my life. Some have touched me benignly, in nurturing care and respect. Others have influenced me, whether through ignorance or malice, in ways I have sensed as negative. But I can come to accept each, even to value each, for a contribution to making me who I am.

It is through the psychological resources of integrity that I am able to discern meaning. I can attest to the meaning of life because I can affirm the meaning of my own life, even in its ambiguities. The acceptance of the particular completeness and wholeness of my own life is integrity realized. With this deep acceptance of self, rooted in now and going back to include the particularity of my personal past, comes the realization that life has meaning because *my life* has meaning. My capacity to reach this synthesis of personal meaning in the face of the ambiguous and contradictory evidence of my own experience is a mark of my movement into full human maturity.

In finding the meaning of my own life, I *insert* meaning into the world. I affirm life's significance from within myself rather than simply in acquiescence to an external system of meaning. I witness that meaning does exist, and I demonstrate how it exists— through the inclination of the human soul to know and to celebrate the spiritual significance of its own life. It is in this sense that meaning enters the world through me. My life is not the whole of human meaning. It is only one facet of a larger constellation. But if my life lacks meaning altogether, so does all of human existence. For the meaning of human existence comes down to my personal struggle to affirm the significance of my own life—in its particularity and limitations—in the face of my realization that I shall soon die.

The affirmation of my own life and the acceptance of my aging, however, do not require that I face the present in a stance of passive adjustment to whatever happens. Resisting attempts by others to shove one aside, lobbying for a flexible national retirement policy, adhering to a physical regime of good diet and exercise, continuing a schedule of activities and commitments—these efforts and others can appropriately mark one's mature years. Here again, as in earlier phases of adult life, both dominance and receptivity will be involved in the successful resolution of the developmental challenges one faces.

INTEGRITY AND DESPAIR

The quality of self-acceptance that becomes possible in mature years has a receptivity about it. Such receptivity is an active response to the particularity and givenness of my own life. It is also an openness to change. If my response to the challenge of aging is to try to hold on to the elements in my earlier life which gave it meaning (at least, such meaning as it has had), then I will distract myself from the tasks of old age. I will immerse myself in the roles and responsibilities of my mid-years and fight against their removal from me. I cannot retain unchanged the forms and functions that provided me security in middle age, but I can try to do so. I can turn away from the invitations of my own aging and attempt to deny its reality. But the denial, ultimately, does not avail. This refusal to accept change and to face the larger questions of personal meaning will only result in stagnation and despair.

Despair, like integrity, is a response to the particularity of my own life. It arises in an inability to find my own life acceptable. It can surface as discontent with the present or as complaint over the shape of the past. These dissatisfactions become despair when accompanied by the realization that there is not enough time left. Death will come too soon to permit me one last chance to make something different—something meaningful—of my life. "Despair expresses the feeling that time is short, too short for the attempt to start another life and to try out alternate roads to integrity" (CS, p. 269; IYC, p. 140).

This despair can also be masked in a cynical bitterness about life in general or harden into a contemptuous criticism of particular institutions and people, those "bearers of meaning" who have failed me or who must be discredited so that my own lack of meaning does not stand out. Or despair may be manifest as an abiding disgust with the pettiness and pretense of life. Disgust and displeasure can be signs of a commitment to a higher vision of life. But when not allied to such superior values, they tend rather to signify an individual's contempt for self. Such disgust is the visible face of a secret despair over the inability to make things different.

Integrity does not eliminate despair. Despair is an appropriate response to my awareness of the limits of my own life and to my consciousness that this life is coming to an end. Not all the possibilities of my life have been realized. I know remorse and regret and guilt in the face of what I have done and what I have failed to do. My death will leave much unattended to—loved ones will be left behind; new possibilities in the world will go unwitnessed. Only an integrity that can be sustained in the face of these realities can bring my life to fruition. Mature integrity remains answerable to despair and regret. Without the tension that is engendered in the struggle to come to terms with despair, self-acceptance remains naive and one's integrity unconvincing. It is the continuing interplay of both positive and negative possibilities that gives my self-acceptance conviction and efficacy. Without this dynamic, my affirmation of life can remain an untested and empty optimism that is of no service to me (since it is likely to crumble under the weight of real despair) nor to others (since its hollowness is sure to sound).

WISDOM: THE FRUIT OF INTEGRITY

When the challenge of personal integrity is successfully resolved, when the impulse toward meaning is in favorable tension with the movement of despair, then there may develop in the aging person that essential strength of character which is wisdom.

Wisdom is manifest in a variety of forms—as ripened wit, as accumulated experience, as mature judgment. Those whom we call wise display an inclusive understanding, a widened empathy, a broadened appreciation of diversity and pluralism. Some older persons give expression to this wisdom in the formulation of a personal philosophy of life to which they can give eloquent testimony. In others this wisdom remains implicit, displayed in their attitudes and actions more than in their words. We are aware of it only in the quiet reassurance we feel when we are with them.

Wisdom is knowledge over time—aware of temporal and cultural variation and not overly impressed with novelty. The wise can cut through to more essential similarities and differences, aware—from history and their own lives—of the consequences of actions. Wisdom is "savvy" about what works with people. It is practiced in living, in loving, in changing. Such wisdom is freed from temporal relativity, but it is not knowledge of "ideal forms." It is rather an accumulated knowledge of the rich particularity of life, a knowledge aware that relativity accompanies any temporally and culturally influenced truth.

The core of this psychological strength of wisdom is a detached yet active concern with life itself, in the face of death (IR, p. 133; IYC, p. 140). Wisdom comes in the realization that my life and my power are bounded by my death, that all life is bounded by death. Yet it is life, not death, that prevails. The recognition of death, my own death, can liberate my concern for life. This realization provides a perspective which relativizes many of the investments and values of my life and yet provides a framework within which to appreciate life's profound meaning. Wisdom's "detached yet active concern" perfects the generative impulses of one's midyears. It is a care for life affirmed in the face of death and the absurdity that death suggests. It does not draw its strength solely from an immersion in the hurly-burly of life, taken seriously and unreflectively as "all there is." The concern which is wisdom can continue to exert its power even in the realization that "all this shall pass," even I shall pass. The discipline of letting go, begun in middle age in the release of one's children and one's work to the dynamism of their own development, gains added strength. Nuanced now by a growing awareness of one's own death, one's sense of responsibility can be transformed in mature renunciation. This renunciation is not (or, at least, not only) a resentful abandonment of my world and my work in the face of the diminishments that accompany aging and death. It goes beyond the bitter awareness of the limits of my power to save even that which I love. The responsible renunciation which can accompany wisdom in mature age is a transcending of self that flowers as a robust faith in the providence and possibilities of life.

Wisdom born in the integrity struggle enables the older person to "envisage human problems in their entirety" (IR, p. 134). This is not a capacity to solve all human problems, or even to understand them fully. But it is an ability to view them, to appreciate them, in their wholeness. The responsible renunciation of which the personality becomes capable in maturity enables me to become somewhat detached emotionally from many situations. My personal investment, which often clouds my perception or blocks my access to certain information, is modified. This more disinterested stance enables me to see a larger picture of many human concerns.

Wisdom can transcend, to some degree, the inevitable diminishments of old age. It is this strength that enables the aged person to maintain confidence in the integrity of personal experience in the face of the decline of bodily and mental functions that can mark the last years. There are real diminishments of old age, especially in its final phases. Much, it is true, can be done to delay and to moderate the negative effects of growing older and being old. Personal planning and flexible social policy can mitigate many of the burdens of aging. But there are real losses in growing old, particularly in the later years of "old-old" age. Decreasing physical vigor is sometimes accompanied by ill health. The loss of loved ones through death narrows the circle of real intimates, those with whom one shares not only the present but the richness of a common past. Physical, financial, and social factors may combine to undermine my independent ability to care for my own life. The recognition and acceptance of an increasing dependency can be the most difficult task of our final years.

The real deprivations of old age, and the feelings of anger and regret that they evoke, can overwhelm the older person. If these are not opposed and ultimately (or at least periodically) overcome by a sense of the wholeness of one's life, by an appreciation of its particularity, by an affirmation of its meaning, then negativity can become the dominant tone, the prevailing mood of one's final years. It is here that the resources of integrity are most keenly tested and the strength of wisdom most required. "Only such integrity can balance the despair of the knowledge that a limited life is coming to a conscious conclusion, only such wholeness can transcend the petty disgust of feeling finished and passed by, and the despair of facing the period of relative helplessness which marks the end as it marked the beginning" (IR, p. 134).

There are many among the old, particularly those in the vigorous period of their sixties and seventies, who experience few of the social diminishments of aging. Some older persons are in occupations where age of itself is not taken as an automatic cause for removal, where one's contribution is either improved with age or clearly not diminished. In our culture these may be persons engaged, for example, in some forms of teaching, writing, politics. They may spend most or even all of their old age in productive positions, without direct experience of many of the physical and social diminishments felt by their age-peers. Others remain vigorous into their seventies in new lifestyles of active leisure or in the context of continuing interaction with their progeny—their adult children and grandchildren, their younger colleagues in "pet" projects or civic concerns. But even these, the culturally "fortunate" aged, must draw upon resources of integrity. For "they, too, eventually join the over-aged who are reduced to a narrowing space-time, in which only a few things, in their self-contained form, offer a last but firm whisper of confirmation" (IR, p. 134).

The need for personal confirmation continues throughout life. But with the mature resources of integrity can come the capacity to stand free, apart from this confirmation. Such transcendence may be elusive, experienced more in a moment of intuition than as a constant conviction. But this depth of wisdom is possible to the human soul. In the moments of this profound awareness my aging, my diminishment, even my death can be transformed.

INTEGRITY AND DEATH

In youth, even through middle age, acceptance of death seems an impossible task. And resistance to the idea of "my own death" and its threat of personal annihilation remains through the aging years. Death is the backdrop against which the drama of the integrity challenge is played. For individuality finds its ultimate test as

I face personal death. The final acceptance of my own life is the acceptance of my death as its finite boundary. Where the lack of integrity prevails, there is a refusal or inability to accept the actual boundaries of life. There is the struggle to overcome one's past and one's inevitable death. Or there is a bitter resignation to their power. Integrity enables me to celebrate the shape that is put to the fluid and ambiguous possibility of life by the fate of my past and my own death.

Erikson counts the fear of death as one of the faces of despair in old age. This fear is less of annihilation than it is of absurdity. Death comes too soon—it will seal the emptiness of my life before I can make sense of it, before I can complete some last desperate attempt to give it meaning. The resources of spirit that are released in the integrity stage can give me the strength to affirm a meaning in my life that transcends my own death. This need not mean that I welcome death (though there is evidence that many older persons do). It need not mean that my final years will not know doubts or regret or fear. But it means that these are not all. With the resources of personal integrity, the completed strength of mature development, I can affirm that, ultimately, death shall not prevail. It is in such "final consolidation" (CS, p. 268) that death loses its sting. For the sting of death is not the loss of life but the loss of meaning.

AGING IN CULTURAL CONTEXT

The emergence of the strengths of mature age depends on favorable cultural conditions. There must be cultural images, social norms, personal models that suggest a favorable outcome is possible in the struggle for personal meaning in old age. There must be values to commend aging as worth the effort. If one's culture has no positive images of aging—if there are no aged heroes, no sages or saints—if there are only senile or bitter old women and sickly or "dirty old men"—the movement into old age will be more difficult.

Mature integration, like the developmental movement of earlier stages, occurs in the context of both personal history and culture. In order to reach maturity, each person, no matter of what culture or class, must come to terms with the series of challenges that describes the sequence of psychological development through the

life course. And the essential form of human maturity, its movements of wisdom and renunciation, will be similar across cultural
differences. But there will develop within cultures and subcultures
particular *styles* of integrity. These distinctive styles will reflect
the culture's images of the human life cycle (whether, for example, it is "better" to be young or to be old), its historical position
(a technological society has a different perception of "young" and
"old" than does agricultural society), and the mosaic of its specific
prescriptions and prohibitions concerning human behavior (how
it resolves, for example, the tension between individual freedom
and group stability).

These cultural images and expectations are the milieu within
which I confront the personal alternatives of meaning and despair. I am more likely to resolve this challenge well if society
holds out positive possibilities for aging and if its institutions support my struggle to find meaning in old age. If the dominant institutions of the culture exclude the aged (through involuntary retirement or inflexible norms of work and productivity) and if
the value institutions—the churches, education, the arts—remain
mute, again I am left alone in the task of discerning the meaning
of growing old. And it is not the aged alone who suffer when the
aged suffer alone. The interpretation that a culture gives to the
final stages of human life has impact not just on its elderly but on
persons in earlier stages of life as well. No matter how society attempts to hide its aged, they are visible. We all know—and possibly fear—what it is like to grow old in America. We have
witnessed how our families, our institutions, our religions, how we
ourselves, treat those who grow old. This information is not lost
on us. It permeates our vision of our own aging and can sap our
strength in the struggle for meaning much earlier in our lives.
"For it can only weaken the vital fiber of the younger generation,"
Erikson notes, "if the evidence of daily living verifies man's prolonged last phase as a sanctioned period of childishness. Any span
of the cycle lived without vigorous meaning, at the beginning, in
the middle, or at the end, endangers the sense of life and the
meaning of death in all whose life stages are intertwined" (IR, p.
133).

The institutions and images of a culture thus can encourage
and support the individual's struggle toward personal integrity.
But these institutions and traditions also depend upon the

strengths of personal character that are evoked in mature adulthood. It is a unique contribution of the elders of any institution, as well as of the culture as a whole, to witness to the possibility of a meaningful old age. Without this personal witness, and the vital perspective it provides on the human life cycle as a whole, the next generation is deprived of the support of an integrated heritage. It is only the old who can offer an assurance that the meanings and symbols of our culture do, in fact, succeed, that they are adequate to the ambiguous report of human existence. And so it is the old who show us our own culture's adequacy. If our tradition can support their movement into mature age, if its symbols can provide interpretations that show the significance of the whole of their lives, then its value is confirmed—not only its value for the aged but its value for us all. Erikson notes: "A civilization and its belief system can be measured by the meaning they give to the full cycle of life, for such meaning (or the lack of it) cannot fail to reach into the beginnings of future generations" (DBL, p. 23).

The interiority of the mid-years is intensified in the integrity stage, with its heightened concern for the meaning of one's life. But this inward movement is complemented—and opposed—by a continuing outward thrust of generativity, a concern for handing on to the next generation an integrated heritage that makes sense and can take its place among the other living traditions of the world. But in this, the wisdom of old age "remains aware of the relativity of all knowledge" (IR, p. 133). This relativity of knowledge does not mean in mature age what it means to the adolescent. It does not mean that none of these traditions of meaning in human life is true, or even that each is equally true. Rather it means that the truth of each is less than complete and is related to the particular experiences from which the truth has emerged or been discerned and affirmed.

The attempt to reach a synthesis of meaning and significance in one's life in mature age is thus part of a larger human effort toward meaning. The traditions of this larger effort are preserved in the religious and other value systems of one's culture. I look to this larger cultural system for its accumulated wisdom—for images and interpretations that can help me to find or give meaning to my own life. In turn, I contribute to the vitality of the culture and its meaning systems by attesting anew to their interpretive power and validity. I must reinterpret and personalize these cultural images. In this they are filled with power for myself and for others. My efforts in late adulthood to deal with meaning become part of a larger cultural effort to create or discern universal values. If my own evaluation is negative, if despair prevails, my effort becomes part of the larger cultural confusion of values. Either stance has implications for my culture and for the vitality of the next generation. My personal struggle for meaning thus becomes a gift to the future, a part of my nurturing care for the next generation.

The generation in which the personal resources of generativity have matured into integrity *cares* for the next generation most profoundly by the witness of its own maturity. This endorsement of life contributes to the development in the next generation of the strengths necessary to face in its own way the ultimate concerns of personal existence. In its responsible resignation, the senior generation can release the next generation from its own domination without leaving scars of exploitation and control. The next generation is left free to face the future in its own way, but supported by the strengths of a vital heritage whose validity is affirmed in the vigor of its elders. Thus the aged "can represent to the coming generation a living example of the 'closure' of a style of life" (IR, p. 134), for "healthy children will not fear life if their elders have integrity enough not to fear death" (CS, p. 269).

EIGHT

To Grow Old
Among Christians

This exercise invites you into your own aging. It may not be an easy experience: Many factors combine in our culture to present aging to us in its most negative light. We will enter mature age here through the imagination. Some simple preliminaries may assist us to gain access to this rich world of personal images.

Find a place and a time that are quiet, where you are not likely to be disturbed. Begin in several moments of gentle recollection—acknowledging, but then letting go, the distractions that press in on you. Let the past be past; let the future remain the future. Rest in the peace of these present moments.

In this experience of quiet, imagine yourself at age seventy-five. First spend some time "getting there." What year is it? How is the world similar to today? How is it different? Then consider yourself at seventy-five. Take some time with this. How does it feel for you to be seventy-five? What do you look like? How do you spend your time? Who are you with at age seventy-five? Where and how do you live?

When your sense of yourself at seventy-five has become real, turn to these questions:
What are the surprises for you in this experience of yourself at seventy-five? How is it different than you had hoped or feared?

What do you like least about being seventy-five? What are its disadvantages for you personally?

What do you like most about being seventy-five? What are its particular advantages for you personally?

There is resonance between the wisdom of human maturity and the wisdom of revelation. Erikson speaks of "the sense in which every human being's Integrity may be said to be religious." Those who take up, in mature age, the struggle to come to some integrated sense of their whole life become involved "in an inner search for, and a wish to communicate with, that mysterious, that Ultimate Other: for there can be no 'I' without an 'Other,' no 'We' without a shared 'Other'" (DBL, p. 11). This inner search is at the heart of Christianity. And at its best the Church is the community in which we may ask these questions of personal significance, unafraid. It is not that we are sure of their answer, nor that we are unawed by their ambiguous threat. We are, rather, together and in hope—expectant that we shall be empowered in the challenge to which these questions invite us and confident that we shall not be alone.

That my life has a significance that transcends my death, that my value is not limited to my achievements, that apparent "losses" may, in fact, be "gains"—these are realizations of psychological maturity. These profound but often fragile intuitions of the human spirit find support in the Christian realities. Jesus' witness to the power of life through death and the symbols of Eucharist and Resurrection add depth and conviction to the hopes of human maturity. In the believing community my personal struggle to respond to the deep questions of my life is illumined by the images of the Tradition and is enheartened by the faith of those with whom I live.

With mature age can come new possibility for spiritual growth. It is in the Christian of advancing years that a lifelong experience of faith and the psychological resources of maturity can combine in an affirmation of the spiritual significance of life. Here one moves beyond a merely deductive and notional assent to meaning (I believe that God has a plan for the world, and therefore my own life makes sense) to an affirmation that evolves from personal experience (I have experienced meaning in my own life; therefore I affirm that human life makes sense).

In every era the Church has been challenged to assist the conversation about meaning, to make available, from the rich store of its heritage, the images and interpretations through which humankind may understand its relationship with God. A part of this challenge today is to expand the ways in which a growing population of older persons may participate in the Christian community.

This participation must include older persons both as contributors to and as recipients of the ministry of the whole community. The community can minister to older persons by taking seriously their needs and experience. As with persons of any age, so with older adults, deeper issues must not be overlooked in a concern for the practicalities that surround daily life. Parishes are to be commended that sponsor programs of home visitation, that offer space for recreational or medical agencies for the elderly, or that provide staff for social services. But beyond these important activities, the parish must not stand mute on the question of meaning. The community must learn to provide for its members of all ages—and especially for those who struggle with issues of integrity—ready access to the powerful Christian understanding of life and death.

Equally, however, the Church today is challenged to develop ways in which mature Christians may contribute to the upbuilding of the community of faith. It is necessary to provide ways and to support ways in which the particular strengths of the older person may be celebrated by the community and put at the service of others. In this chapter we shall discuss in turn both of these: the ministry to meaning in mature age, and the contribution of the mature Christian to the believing community.

CHRISTIAN MEANING
IN MATURE AGE

There are, perhaps, questions of aging that do not arise until one's later years. But the most significant issues of mature age are questions that attend human life over much of its course. Of what value am I? What does a human life mean? How am I to deal with suffering, with change and loss? Why must I die? These are the central questions of personal meaning. Through much of our lives we may conspire with the everyday purposes and preoccupations of our culture to distract ourselves from their urgency. But the questions remain—to inspire us in moments of solitude, to haunt our moments of despair. In the mature years of later adulthood, as we have seen, these questions of integrity arise to prominence. The aging person must affirm personal meaning against a more immediate realization that "I, too, shall die."

The images and convictions of Christian Tradition can illumine this struggle for personal meaning. We will return to three challenges to meaning that are central to personal aging, to discern the ways in which Christianity may help us understand the ambiguous experience of growing older and being old. The challenges are: establishing a sense of self-worth less dependent upon productivity or role; reaching a deeper acceptance of one's own life; and coming to terms with the diminishments and losses of aging.

ESTABLISHING A BASIS OF SELF-WORTH

In periods of reflection and in prayer we can come to sense the extent to which illusions and masks make up our lives. Times of crisis or ecstasy challenge us to lay these aside, to accept ourselves as we really are and to confront life as it is. This is the invitation to authenticity—to give up all that is superficial in order that we may find our truest self, to die to the things of this world in order that we might live to the things of God. In those moments—however fleeting—when we experience such authenticity, we come to sense the power of integrity. Mature age is the season of this power. The older person is brought by choices within and forces without to that point of growth at which integrity ripens. As I grow old, I am challenged to lay aside the illusions I have needed in my youth. They may have served me once—even well—but they serve me no longer. I am asked to lay aside, as well, many of the fragile advantages that have contributed to my sense of worth.

Now, with most of my life behind me, I face the question of its significance. This can be an anxious question. As I move into mature age, I feel myself being removed from many of the sources to which I have customarily turned to find an answer. Earlier in my life I may have depended on my physical presence—beauty, vigor, strength—to provide some sense of personal significance. Physical changes during middle age and aging bring into question that part of my identity that depends on physical prowess. I can, of course, care for my body. Through exercise, diet, and health care I can compensate for some of the effects of aging and I can delay others. But these physical changes associated with aging are inevitable. My body will become different as I grow old.

I may turn to my productive involvement in the world or to my realm of social responsibilities for confirmation of my current value and long-term significance. Again changes, both socially induced and personally chosen, alter these sources of personal meaning. In aging, my productivity may decrease in some jobs or my motivation in my work may change. I may be required to retire or to shift my work responsibility. Or I may choose to do so for positive reasons (I want to spend my time differently) or negative (I experience declining vigor or poor health). I see myself replaced by others—by persons who are younger than I rather than by persons more experienced. Does my accumulated experience, then, that factor which is my particular advantage now as I age, count for nothing? These changes affect the meaning I derive from being a productive person. And my relationship to what I have produced also changes. The works of my hands are less under my control. The meaning I have achieved in what I have produced, while not denied, is nevertheless altered.

I may have gained much personal meaning from the relationships in my life—those who love me and whom I have loved, those who need me and whom I need, those who support me and whom I have supported. Again there is movement and change as I grow older. My spouse may die; friends may move away; my adult children need me in different ways than they did earlier. My relation to my colleagues may be dramatically altered by my retirement or a change in residence. Here again I do not have a firm or unchanging criterion for evaluating the worth of my own life, past or present.

Reputation, accomplishment, beauty, influence, affection, wealth—these have been important sources of my self-esteem. They have helped me to know and to accept myself. In my deepest moments, though, I have been troubled by their power over me. I have sensed how vulnerable I am to their loss. What if I fail? What if I lose? What if they do not like me? . . . Where will I be then? But surely I must be more than just the sum of the circumstances of my life. Surely there must be within myself and my experience of life other sources from which I draw my sense of who I truly am.

This realization that "I am more than what I do" is a critical insight of human maturity. It is a central conviction of every religious tradition as well. Christianity proclaims that the real basis of one's worth lies beyond one's accomplishments, even beyond good works. Ultimately it is God's love that grounds human dignity and the mature sense of self-worth. God does not love me because I am good; rather, I am able to be good because God loves me. And God's love is unconditioned. It is both unmerited and unmeritable. It does not *depend* on what I do or who I am; it constitutes these.

The Christian affirmation of personal worth is relevant not only to the aged, but its power is tested in a particular way in one's old age. To affirm God's love as a source of my worth when my life is going well, when there are several other sources of positive evaluation to which I can turn, is itself a movement of grace. It is a deeper challenge to affirm the primacy of this love when the other sources of value in my life become unsure. It is these times that test the power of Christianity to illumine the shadows of human life, to give meaning, if not release.

REACHING A DEEPER ACCEPTANCE OF SELF

The sense of integrity that is the special strength—the virtue—of mature age involves a deep acceptance of oneself. This is an acceptance of one's particularity, one's finiteness and limitation. Such acceptance moves beyond simple acquiescence toward appreciation and celebration of my unique, though limited, self. This profound encounter with myself can be a movement of transcendence. In a deep acceptance of my own particularity I can experience an expansion beyond the limits of self. I can reach an awareness that I am one with humankind, with all creation. Christianity proclaims a yet more profound paradox—that this conscious acceptance of my own finiteness is a path to personal salvation. The lives of its saints witness to the power that is released as one assents to, even celebrates, one's weakness. The Christian can come, with Paul, even to "boast of my weaknesses" (2 Cor. 12:9): for these are themselves reminders that "it is no longer I who live, but Christ who lives in me" (Gal. 2:20).

One of the manifestations of the integrity of mature age is the ability to defend one's own lifestyle. We can see evidence of this psychological impulse in the immigrant grandfather's desire to share with his grandchildren stories about life in the old country.

It emerges in the older woman's concern that her grandchildren be imbued with knowledge and respect for family traditions; in the retired pastor's testimony to the value of devotional practices of the pre–Vatican II Church. There is an appreciation that my life, in its particularity and peculiarity, has been good. My lifestyle has contributed to who I am today and to the meaning my life has had over its course. It is one of the ways in which human life can be lived meaningfully.

Maturity in the integrity stage appreciates the relativity of my own lifestyle. It is only one of the ways of being human, but it is a good way. It has worked for me and can, I believe, work for others. Immaturity in the integrity stage is defensive. I must insist on the value of my lifestyle and I must bring you to value it as well. My own conviction is not sufficient to assure me that my life has had meaning; I need outside reinforcement. I cannot afford to have my lifestyle be just one among several. Its worth to me does not come from within my experience of it. I must have its worth (and, therefore, my worth) acknowledged from outside as the only valuable or the most valuable style.

In either case there is a willingness to profess and to defend one's lifestyle. But a different feeling predominates in each. In the mature form I defend my lifestyle so that I may pass on to the next generation the "good news" of how to make the perilous but exciting journey of life. My defense of myself may be, in part, self-verification, but it is in good measure disinterested care for the future. My witness to my own lifestyle is part of my larger effort at handing on to the next generation those values I have known. In its immature form, it is the need for self-verification that predominates. It is myself whom I must convince as well as others.

Integrity is the personal resource that makes pluralism possible. One can recognize the value in other persons and other value systems and assent to the partiality of one's own values. Maturity brings an ease in accepting the relativity of one's choices, in acknowledging the positive and negative aspects of both one's own lifestyle and the lifestyles of others. But in this maturity one's appreciation of relativity is coupled with a capacity for personal choice, and for commitment to the particular in the face of other possibilities.

With the awareness of the goodness of my lifestyle comes an emotional appreciation of my own goodness, in my particularity, in my final years. This sense of personal integrity is possible earlier in life, and is needed whenever pluralism and diversity are real. But it becomes a fully developed resource and a habitual virtue in one's old age.

The religious community ministers to this critical issue of self-acceptance by providing that attentive support which encourages its older members to tell the particular story of their personal and generational life with God. This can be done in individual counseling sessions, in support groups established in neighborhood or nursing-home settings, and in the context of adult religious education and group prayer. The religious community can also provide the occasions in which these stories can become part of the religious activity of the whole community. We shall spend more time with this ministry of mature Christians to the community in our discussion of the past and religious anamnesis.

FACING RENUNCIATION AND LOSS

A central movement of human maturity is the repeating dynamic of accepting and then relinquishing, of caring and letting go. The letting go begun in generativity, in the release and transcendence of one's work and in the altruistic concern for nurturing new life on its own terms, gains added nuance in the mature years. For Americans today, as we have seen before, growing older is often accompanied by changes in income, residence, and lifestyle. For many there is also the experience of loss—of one's spouse, of cherished friends and companions, of status and vigor and health. Not all these changes need be, or are, experienced as negative. And the effects of many of the losses of aging can be lessened by personal planning and effective social policy. But change and loss are part of human aging. Diminishment and death are its companions.

As human maturity ripens in the psychological strengths of integrity and wisdom, the older person becomes capable of an acceptance of self and an appreciation of life that transcend the diminishments that are inevitable in advanced age, transcend even the awareness of death. In old age, I can learn to let go even my life.

Such letting go is central to personal maturity; it is at the heart of Christian spirituality as well. At the core of Christian mysticism is *kenosis*, the spirituality of emptying oneself. This religious image finds forceful expression in Paul's description of Jesus, who "emptied himself, taking the form of a servant" (Phil. 2:7). The religious invitation is clear. I must empty myself of the distracting ambitions and false sense of value that are obstacles to spiritual awareness. I must let go my control of my life as a prerequisite to undertaking the journey toward God.

In Christianity this asceticism of self-emptying is not limited to the old. It is a challenge offered to all. But in this perspective the losses of aging need not be experienced solely as negative. Physical loss, social loss, financial loss can be interpreted, as well, as part of a spiritually significant discipline of emptying and letting go. The Christian is thus invited to recognize the religious possibilities hidden within even those aspects of human aging that obviously do harm. For the Christian, then, there may be *more* to the diminishments of aging than simply their negative effect. These losses can serve to remind the believer how fragile all human life is. This insight into human contingency is central in religious traditions of both East and West. It grounds the Christian insistence on the importance of immediate experience, "the sacrament of the present moment." "In obtaining this fullness of the present," as Sidney Callahan and Drew Christiansen remark, "a discipline is imposed, as in old age: one must be removed from power, be divested of external social roles, and turn away from the world's claims" (1974, p. 12).

In facing and accepting the real diminishments of aging, the older person is led to see things as they really are. The deprivations and losses of advancing age are opportunities to divest oneself of the illusions and false securities of life, which often serve as distractions from the life of the spirit. Letting go these distractions, one is able to live more fully in the present, to appreciate life as it is. Thus the quest for spiritual awareness is continued, even brought to maturity, in the challenge of the acceptance of one's old age.

These ideals of acceptance are potentially powerful vehicles of religious awareness. We must take care at the political level that they do not deteriorate into excuses for our society's less-than-adequate response to its aging members. Many of the negative aspects of growing old in America can, and should, be changed. Flexible retirement policies, financial security in mature age, preventive medicine and health-care delivery, continuing participation of older Americans in civic life—these issues must be addressed with more creativity than American public policy has shown to date. Religious images, used to delay or divert this public discussion, are misused.

THE CONTRIBUTION
OF MATURE CHRISTIANS
TO THE COMMUNITY OF FAITH

It is not enough for us to "care for the needs of the elderly," even their religious needs. As Christians we do want to care for those in need, and so this phase of a response to older persons is essential—but it is not enough. Our stance to the elderly must be that which we assume toward any other: a stance that begins with inclusion. We must first invite the elderly to be with us, and then move toward full community through that respectful dynamic in which we expect both to give to and to receive from one another.

We cannot include older persons unless we see our deep similarity. So a most important contribution toward our ministry to the elderly is to come to terms with our own aging—the parts of it to which we look forward and the parts that we fear—aging in both its promise and its terror. If we do this, we are likely to be less susceptible to the displacement through which we turn our anxiety about our own growing older into guilt or fear of those among us who are already old, who remind us of parts of ourselves and of our lives from which we would rather hide.

Our response to the elderly is also limited if we see them simply as needy, as potential recipients of our generosity. This is a problem, first, because it prohibits that mutuality which is prerequisite for community. Second, it is a problem because it makes the aged potential exhausters of our resources—whether of money, or time, or creativity, or emotion. If they only take and never give back to us, we are not likely to consider them, over the long term, as deserving of our respect.

In addition, if our only image of the elderly is of their need, we are likely to contribute to making them needy. If we have only negative categories for the old—categories of dependence and weakness and suffering—we are likely to meet only aged of these kinds. This is so either because only older persons with needs will be drawn to us or sought out by us (others remaining "invisible" to us) or because we will turn the elderly with whom we do relate into needy persons. Many elderly persons are in an ambiguous social position—moving from one image of themselves toward some new image, as yet unclear. If we comunicate to them only our own negative expectations of them as older persons, if we do not reinforce their ability to make of aging something powerful and graceful, if we anticipate only negative effects, to them and to us, of their growing old—then we will contribute to the likelihood that their movement into old age will fit these negative stereotypes.

So it is important that we anticipate the strengths of the elderly. It is important both for ourselves (in terms of preparation for our own aging) and for them that we can understand—can imagine—the potential and actual contributions of mature Christians to us and to the whole community of faith. We are not likely to devise creative ways for the active and contributing inclusion of older persons in the Christian community unless we conceive of the elderly as powerful and graced with strengths which are of value to us and to others.

First, then, we must accept our own aging. Then, we must believe in and articulate the strengths of the elderly for the believing community. We must assist others (even the elderly) to come to a sense of the actual and possible strengths of those who are aging and who are old. Then, together with the elderly, we will have to devise respectful, expectant, and appropriate ways for this contribution to be made within this particular community.

Older persons, many with more flexible free time now than earlier in their adult lives, can be involved in a variety of self-help and service projects—developing a credit union, volunteering for hospital and home visitation for the sick and infirm, staffing service agencies, helping with the managerial tasks of the parish, planning social and recreational activities. But beyond this there is the imperative that the Church provide and encourage the inclusion of mature believers in its religious and liturgical life. This will require an examination of the particular contribution of older persons to the religious tasks of the local Church—their role in witnessing to the life of faith, of validating the adequacy of Christian symbols to the ambiguous experience of the whole of a human life.

It is to mature Christians in their later years that the rest of us must turn to learn if Christianity "works." It is in their conviction, accumulated and personalized over the course of their individual lives, that our own hopes will find reinforcement. True, they cannot believe for us, but their belief before us is a powerful witness. Its efficacy comes from their having "fought the good fight," having "finished the race" (2 Tim. 4:7). From this perspective their words carry added weight.

Realizing this ministry of mature Christians will entail developing ways in which both the struggle and the affirmation of mature age may be shared with the believing community. We will offer two examples here: the acceptance of one's past in religious *anamnesis*, and the sacrament of aging.

THE PAST AND RELIGIOUS ANAMNESIS

A common stereotype of the older person is as one who "lives in the past." This phrase is used somewhat indiscriminately to signify a variety of behaviors. It sometimes refers to a predilection for explaining present happenings by reference to earlier events, for evaluating current situations against the standard of a historical perspective or, even, "how things have always been done." In other instances it points to a tendency among some older persons to recall and recount the details of their earlier life. On some occasions such preoccupation with one's personal past can be problematic—it can signify a refusal to deal effectively with the present or, in extreme cases, manifest a deeper physical or psychological deterioration. But in most cases an increasing interest in one's past in the mature years is important and developmentally sound.

The past is a category of particular significance in mature age. The acceptance of one's own past is central to the psychological challenge of integrity. And it is through personal memories—the dynamic of recollection, reliving, and storytelling—that this acceptance is achieved. Gerontologists speak of this psychologically significant process of reminiscence as the "life review"—"a naturally occurring, universal mental process characterized by the progressive return to consciousness of past experiences" (Butler, 1968, p. 487).

"Probably at no other time in life," Butler remarks, "is there as potent a force toward self-awareness operating as in old age" (p.

495). Such powerful self-awareness can be a gift to the community of believers as well as a force for personal integration. This recovery of memories, this recollection of one's past, can be understood religiously as *anamnesis.* Christians, "calling to mind" the death and resurrection of Jesus Christ, celebrate in the Eucharist this past event's saving power in the present. This celebration occurs in response to Jesus' request that it be done "in remembrance of me" (Luke 22:19). Believers of every faith are empowered by the memories, made present, of God acting in their past. These recollections recover the gracefulness of past events and serve to integrate the many pasts of a person's life with the present.

In those cases where the believing community (the family, the parish, the prayer group, the religious house) can support its older members in their life-review, can share in the experience with them and proclaim its religious significance, the community is itself enlivened by the witness of faith. The personal past of those who believe with us and before us is the "deposit of faith" of our community. It is a record of God's action and provident care among us, concretely, in the world today.

There are various ways in which this religious *anamnesis* may be supported and celebrated among us. We may each learn better to listen to the stories of those older persons who are deeply a part of our own lives—our parents, our family, our friends and colleagues. We may understand this ministry of listening as an important part of our religious presence with the elderly in our communities, in nursing homes and hospitals. (And, then, acquire the skills to enable us to listen well: attentively, respectfully, religiously.) We may plan creatively to include the testimony of mature believers in the liturgical life of the parish. The celebration of baptism, for example, may appropriately include the active participation of the child's grandparents along with other "senior believers" in the community, as witnesses to the lifelong power of the faith into which the child is invited. The solemnities of Holy Week and the Easter season are rich in the symbols of life through death and of the transformation of human purposes in God's loving but mysterious plan. The respectful inclusion of older persons in visible and vocal roles in these ceremonies can deepen the significance of these powerful images. In these ways and others we seek as a believing community to trace the movement of God among us. And we attest to and strengthen our shared belief in the ultimate religious significance of each life. Thus, under the guidance of our religious elders, the Christian community can come to believe more deeply and to proclaim that "the life cycle, seen as a whole, is—perhaps—a revelation" (DBL, p. 12).

THE SACRAMENT OF AGING

The concentrated religious actions of symbol and ritual are central in Christian tradition. The Church is visible and powerful in sacramental ministry—as it baptizes into Christian fellowship, confirms to Christian action, and celebrates the Lord in the breaking of the bread. One influential interpretation of this symbolic activity, as we noted in Chapter Two, is built on an understanding of rites of passage. In this understanding, a sacrament is a rite (a symbolic activity of a community) which focuses on a critical and dangerous time, a moment of passage, in a person's life. This may be a passage into life (baptism), into marital intimacy and commitment (matrimony), or into death (sacrament of the dying). The rites associated with ordination focus on the passage from one role or identity into another. The crucial point is that the person entering upon this point of passage is in danger: He or she is leaving one identity behind and is, in that exposed moment of passage, "between" identities. A sacrament is the symbolic and public act of a community (feeling itself, as the Christian community does, empowered by God) which has as its intent the empowering of the individual through the crisis of this dangerous passage.

It is only in the past century that the shape of a new stage of adult growth has appeared. Increased longevity has added several decades to adulthood, decades during which we may enjoy and contribute to life in a different mode. Retirement is not just a threshold of sickness and death; it can represent the transition into a new and important stage of adult maturity. Both this stage of maturity and one's passage into it invite a new ministerial response from the Church. We will discuss this passage into the final stage of adulthood in terms of a sacrament of aging.

By "retirement" we signify here the general phenomenon of moving from an active, specific, and role-related identity in the community to a stage where one is relatively less active and has been retired from a specific role in the community. Let us look a bit closer at the passage involved. At retirement I experience my identity to be taken away by the society. I am no longer a lawyer, or a grocer, or a secretary; I am now retired. The former roles each enjoyed very specific definition, quite precise indicators of one's value (such as amount of money earned, status in the community, etc.). The retiring person dies to these signs (or even, proofs) of personal identity and worth; she or he passes from this way of life, filled with indicators of value and usefulness, into another way of life—where all the social indicators suggest uselessness and non-identity. The society which had taught me to respond to the question "Who are you?" with the answer "I am a lawyer," "I am a grocer," "I am a secretary," now leaves me no valuable answer. It would seem that it is precisely such a critical passage which calls for a sacramental response from the ministering Church.

What are the responses of a religious community, sacramental or not, to a person retired from social identity and usefulness? One response, which arises from the seduction of the culture rather than from the riches of a religious tradition, is to invent substitute roles for the elderly: Give them something to do (anything!) around which they might fabricate a substitute identity and escape a sense of uselessness.

But there is another response which has its roots more firmly in religious awareness. This response is to celebrate the uselessness of the person. Through many centuries and cultures, as we noted above, religious traditions have rebelled against the identifying of a person by the criterion of usefulness to the society. A deep sense that a person does not earn his or her way into a relationship with God, that societal and role credentials fail somehow to establish personal worth, permeates Christian spirituality. One does not *depend* on such things as social status, salary, or credentials to guarantee one's relationship with God. Yet despite the best insights of many religious traditions, societies and cultures insidiously convince us that it is by our usefulness that we are to be judged and are to judge ourselves.

The religious critique of this "worldly" attitude, as we noted earlier in this chapter, often takes the form of an emphasis on emptying. The objective is always to empty out of oneself those false bases of self-esteem and to counter the unending efforts to validate oneself, to finally accumulate the credentials that prove to everyone (though we ourselves are the last to be convinced) our worth. The point here is that the event of retirement performs this very act. It empties out of a person's life perhaps the most sturdy crutch of self-worth, one's social role and usefulness. In this moment of stripping away, of death to a former style of life, the Church's ministry must not be to substitute ersatz identities, thus prolonging the irreligious game, but to celebrate this emptying. The Church can assure the individual that this loss of social identity does not mean death in the religious sense. While it cares for the retired individual (with economic support if necessary; with emotional support, which is always necessary), it announces the good news of one's uselessness. The aging person now stands as a sign to the community of what the community always believed even if it could not always live—the Christian is not justified or validated by work, by achievements or credentials. Society serves, ironically, a religious function by stripping the individual of social role and identity; the Church has only to embrace this event in an interpretation of its religious significance, assuring the person that one *does not have to do anything* to be a part of this community. He or she does not have to constantly "earn" the respect of others.

The religious community will certainly include roles and activities for its mature members—but *not* as ways for them to earn respect. The community will make use of the many talents of the aging, but not to prove their usefulness. Along with economic assistance, counseling, and emotional support, the religious community will celebrate this stage in life, celebrate its specific gracefulness: its *kenosis* of credentials and its praise of uselessness.

Thus among the educational and supportive rites of passage can be included the ritual or liturgical recognition of the person's new status in the community. Scriptural references to wisdom in old age can be used to shape a ritual in which the older person is initiated into this new stage in life, as the community acknowledges both its perils and its special opportunities. Such a ritual will explicitly invite these mature believers to bear witness to the religious meaning of their lives and of the Christian life. With such recognition of their new religious status, older persons will stand within the Christian community as signs—as sacraments—of a larger truth: that life is, at base, a gift; that we do not earn our way. Through the sacrament of aging, and the communal and educational actions that support it, the mature person is helped to celebrate this stage of life: to move beyond despair or a compulsive living in the past into an appreciation of the present—beginning, in anticipation, the "uselessness" of an unending life with God.

Conclusion

THE DYNAMICS OF ADULT
MATURING REVISITED

Throughout the discussions of this book we have seen that the invitations of a life with God are not foreign to the challenges of psychosocial growth. Psychological development and religious growth are not enemies. Yet interpretations of these two paths of growth have sometimes made them appear quite alien to each other.

Religious growth has often been portrayed as necessitating withdrawal from the world and hatred of self. Retreat and rejection predominated over development and integration. Such growth had as its ideal the attainment of perfection—a nondevelopmental plateau to be reached by mysterious means, rather unrelated or even inimical to processes of "natural development." Holiness as the goal of religious maturity was often epitomized in eccentric personalities—persons whose careers departed from rather than illuminated the patterned challenges of human growth.

The result of this orientation toward religious growth was twofold: the disassociation of the two tasks of psychological and religious development, and the mystification of religious growth. Religious maturity and holiness took on increasingly interiorized and individualistic shape, becoming more exceptional than expectable. For many adult Christians this mystification has been disconcerting. As contemporary believers we often realize that we are not the stable adults that we had once hoped to be. Often we sense ourselves to be not very "religious." But we find ourselves, in response to the challenges of adult life, getting better at loving and working. In this book we have argued that hidden in the challenges of psychological development are the agenda of a contemporary Christian spirituality. Getting better at loving and working is thus, for the Christian, a religious task.

In the mores of contemporary America, loving and working are highly competitive endeavors. In both, we learn early to play to win. But maturity, both psychological and religious, involves not so much winning as learning to prevail. "Prevailing" falls somewhere between an avoidance of contact (loving and working are, after all, contact sports) and the domination and fierce control required for conquest. Maturity lies in freedom from both these extremes: the fear that inhibits encounter, and the drive that impells one toward the isolation of being a sole victor.

If maturity has much to do with learning how to prevail, and to prevail *with* others, it also involves becoming good at losing. The pattern of natural growth as well as of religious development offers the paradoxical invitation "Unless a grain of wheat falls into the earth and dies, it remains alone; but if it dies, it bears much fruit" (John 12:24). "He who finds his life will lose it, and he who loses his life for my sake will find it" (Matt. 10:39).

Cultural biases concerning competition provoke real fear of defeat. But losing can be subject to a more mature and mellow interpretation. Crossan notes the connection between life and a "game." In a game (as distinct from a sport) one competes not against other contestants but against the limitations of the game itself. Thus a game is played out in a context of "partial and disciplined success, always mixed with failure." Crossan argues that the game constitutes· "a very serious practice session for life and death. . . . It is a cautious experience of the necessity of limit and the inevitability of death" (1975, p. 17). The dynamic of loss and gain which patterns adult growth teaches us how to play well at loving and working; maturity allows us to accept the failures and even to savor the limitations experienced in our own efforts at intimacy and generativity.

ACTIVE AND PASSIVE MASTERY: AN ASCETICISM OF LETTING GO

We mature as adults by learning how to prevail and how to lose. A dynamic in human development that facilitates this learning is the dialectic of control and letting go or of active and passive mastery.

Adult life is pre-eminently a life of agency. Leaving behind the dependence and relative impotence of childhood, adults exercise themselves in creative and productive acts. Adults *do*; they initiate and perform. We develop the skills and strengths that give a relative mastery of ourselves and of the environment. With energy and control we not only respond to events but establish our world and our roles in it.

Complementing this active mastery, in which agency and control are so crucial, is the maturing adult's ability to receive, to undergo, and experience. In intimacy relationships, whether in love or work, we grow by being able actively to attend to others and to risk alteration by letting them into our life. It is this attentiveness which marks a mature openness to others, to God, and to the dreams and intuitions that come to us from within. This capacity for openness is often sorely tested in a crisis, when the voices to which we attend can carry unexpected and even painful news, when the invitation is to growth through the experience of loss. It is this adult strength, however, which allows us to achieve that crucial task of adult maturation—letting go.

Letting go is a psychological ability with a rich tradition in religious history. In the Christian tradition this central act of mature self-denial is reflected in the religious ideals of renunciation and self-abandonment. A contemporary spirituality will recognize the religious invitation of renunciation and self-denial in the psychological challenge to let go of the firm hold on one's identity in the risk of intimate encounter and to let go of children and other creations in mature generativity. In the critical transitions of adult life some part of my self—an accustomed, familiar, and even cherished part—must be let go if I am to grow. This is renunciation, not out of masochistic or macabre motive, but in response to the invitation of growth. We find that when we cannot let go, when we do not pass through a crisis and become reconciled to a new way of life, we fail not only as adults but as Christians. We lessen our ability to love and to work well.

This ability to let go, balanced by the ability to express oneself powerfully in life, is tested and gradually developed in adulthood. Learning that I am enhanced rather than destroyed by letting go in love, I can approach the later tasks of letting go with more confidence and, for the Christian, more virtue. In my mid-years this virtue will be tested and strengthened again, as I learn to let go of my children and the projects of my adult responsibility, aware that they will change even as I give up my control over them. This developed strength will assist me in the transition into mature age, where I am challenged to let go of former signs of self-worth: my career, my physical ability, my influence. And the prospect of my death will invite an even more radical surrender. I will be asked to set aside my final claim to my own life and to commit to the loving providence of the Lord both my achievements and the many things that I have left undone. The humanist is challenged in this last passage to believe in the process of life; the Christian believes with Christ that this loss, like the other frightening and confusing losses that have gone before, will lead—ultimately—to life.

Thus for the psychologically and religiously maturing person, the sense of agency and control alternates with the ability to receive and to let go. When an adult life is viewed as a story, this dynamic of control and letting go, of active and passive mastery, can be translated as the alternation of myth and parable.

Myth here stands for the larger story, the interconnected meanings that give direction and purpose to life. In this sense the Christian myth becomes the story of God's actions with this group of believers. A part of the larger Christian story or myth is the story of an individual person, the plot (*mythos*) that structures a particular religious biography. The exercises suggested in this book are intended to assist adults to listen to their own story and become more familiar with its plot. For the Christian this means a deeper awareness of how God has moved in and has guided this life, how this is a religious story.

Myth then is the story that our lives tell. Yet we know that an adult life is not a smoothly unfolding story but one in which failure and contradictions occur. Periods of crisis disrupt and change the direction of the plot, challenging the continuity, control, and agency that are so much a part of an adult story. In elaborating a theology of story Crossan (1975) opposes "myth," which builds a world of meaning, to "parable," which attacks or challenges this myth.[1] Parables (think of the confusing parables in the Gospels) display a fascinating parallel to adult crises and passage. "The sur-

1. Crossan suggests five elements of a story in its relationship to world: myth, apologue, action, satire, and parable. "Myth establishes world. Apologue defends world. Action investigates world. Satire attacks world. Parable subverts world" (p. 59). A parable operates within a myth, inviting its re-examination.

face function of parable is to create contradiction within a given situation of complacent security . . ." (p. 57). Like a crisis, a parable breaks into the ordinary flow of a life story. Similar to an unexpected or unscheduled crisis, "parable is always a somewhat unnerving experience" (p. 56). And yet like a crisis, a parable—negatively breaking into the narrative of such a story—invites a person to reflection and growth. "Like satire, parable is intrinsically negative. It is in fact the dark night of story, but precisely therein and thereby can it prepare us for the experience of transcendence" (p. 60).

LIFE CHOICES: PARTICULARITY AND PLURALISM

A second dynamic of psychological and religious development in adult life is growth from the general to the particular, expressed in specific and specifying life choices. In earliest adulthood everything is possible; enthusiasm unencumbered by failure or by the experience of personal limitation engages the young adult in a variety of relationships and plans for the future. This universal concern and enthusiasm is most appropriate at this point in life: Such idealism makes generous and energetic self-investments possible. A young adult too conscious of the limits in life and the drawbacks hidden in choices appears prematurely old and out of phase.

The challenge of adult growth is to focus one's possibilities into specific choices; out of life's endless potential a person is asked to make quite particular choices about future directions of loving and working. In the early stages of adult life I am invited to focus my general concern for many others into a love for a few concrete individuals.[2] During the twenties I am also testing a personal dream and its potential meaning for my lifework. Here too choices must be made: Any specific choice means limitation. To choose *this* job for the future—as to choose this partner—means to lose other possibilities. Everything is not possible after all. Matu-

2. Vaillant's research points to the middle and late twenties as the period during which, most commonly, adults make this delimiting choice in response to the challenge of intimacy. For Vaillant the commune is a contemporary symbol of a generalized intimacy commitment that, developmentally, must be grown beyond: "At least in our culture, if the commune prevents loneliness before 30, it perpetuates it afterwards" (1977, p. 215).

rity combines a recognition of this somewhat sobering fact with
an affirmation of specific choices and their goodness. I can recognize that the worth of my choices is not jeopardized by their particularity and limitation. As I mature, I may find my spouse to be
flawed and my chosen career to have surprising limitations. And
both of these limitations have intimate connections with a growing sense of my own limits. Maturity occurs in my appreciation of
the *fit* of these limitations—the particular adult who I am finds
fitting expression with this particular partner and in this specific
work.

Failure at adult living appears to be related not to these limitations in self, spouse, and job—since these are experienced by
everyone—but to my response to limitation. An acute awareness
of the limitations of an intimacy commitment may prevent me
from making any such choice; uncommitted to any *ones*, I will find
the movement toward maturity more difficult. Interested in a variety of jobs, I may be unable to choose any one; again, inability to
choose and commit myself makes it difficult to give concrete and
sustained expression to my creativity and generativity. Adult
growth is thus frustrated in two ways: by the inability to commit
oneself to particular choices, or by the inability to sustain these
commitments in the face of their particularity and limitations.

This dynamic of growth from the general to the particular
reaches a critical point for many in the mid-life transition or crisis.
A growing sense of limits in my love life and work life may now
be heightened by a sudden sense of personal mortality. Death becomes a more immediate and specific concern than it had been. I
begin to realize more concretely that my own life has a limit, that
its termination is no longer simply a vague and unreal possibility.
For many adults, as we have noted, the mid-years become a time
of re-evaluation and reconciliation. Specific choices in love and
work have brought me to this point in life. The crisis here is most
ambiguous—the re-evaluation of these life choices in the light of a
reawakened dream and sense of limits may indicate a significant
change to be made or may invite me to a reaffirmation of these
commitments.

Developmentally, the mid-life crisis of the limits and its review
of one's life choices challenges an adult to an affirmation of *this
life* with all its limits. By coming to a deeper acceptance of my
own life with all its particularity and fragility, I prepare for the

next challenge of life, that of integrity. If a deeper affirmation of my own limited life, with its earlier potential only partly realized, rehearses me for the tasks of integrity, failure to achieve this psychological and religious reconciliation can leave me restless, nostalgic (for what might have been in my life), or accusatory (blaming others for not coming up to my expectations).

The maturity which accompanies a more thorough self-acceptance at mid-life also allows for a new appreciation of pluralism. In younger adulthood pluralism may simply have meant letting others "do their own thing" out of a reluctance to confront their differing values. Later, with a maturing sense of my own particularity and limits, I more clearly recognize how others can be different from me. These differences now appear less as a threat to my life choices ("Which one of us is right?") and more as an instance of another way to love and work. A person who remains unreconciled to her or his own particularity and its goodness will have difficulty tolerating other particular persons living out other limited life choices.

SELF-TRANSCENDENCE

A third dynamic common to psychological and religious growth is self-transcendence. The phrase "psychological growth" has for some a narcissistic nuance, suggesting intense self-interest and a focus on individual fulfillment at whatever expense. This caricature of psychological development is in striking opposition to notions of religious growth as dependent on self-denial and service to others. But, as we have seen in earlier chapters, self-transcendence stands as a challenge in both psychological maturation and religious development. Self-transcendence is a capacity which emerges gradually in the life schedule. An infant is necessarily self-centered and need-oriented. In adolescence an important self-concern continues as one struggles toward a somewhat stable sense of self. When such a resolution is not achieved, an adult has no consistent self to invest in love and work, no self to give away.

In early adulthood the first powerful invitation to self-transcendence occurs. Even if a love relationship is begun for reasons of self-centered concern, a person is continually invited to go beyond this orientation into a union which will change the self. Mature intimacy becomes possible when I can broaden my own concerns and feelings in empathy with others—feeling what another is feeling. Self-transcendence lies at the heart of such intimacy, whether symbolized in ec-static (standing outside of oneself) sexual experience or in the offspring which result from and transcend an intimacy relationship.

In the mid-years of adult life a person's family and job increase this invitation to go beyond self in care. This generative care is further refined as I learn to let go the control (of children, of job) that formerly modified it. Such self-transcendence can be experienced as well in becoming a genuine mentor—caring for younger persons without my own agenda interfering, without trying to fashion them in my own image.

The penultimate passage in life, the transition into mature age, holds yet another challenge of self-transcendence. Aging persons are asked to care for persons and communities whose future they will not share. Someone who has failed the challenge of self-transcendence will be uninterested in working for something with no direct reward. Adults who have negotiated the task of integrity and affirmed the meaning, not only of their own life but of the human venture, will be able to reach beyond selfish concerns and nostalgia and continue to give of themselves.

There are for the Christian powerful images to support this call to self-transcendence. The first is that of Moses (and his generation) looking to a promised land that they would not enjoy. His generation—by their efforts and response to Yahweh's guidance—made the land possible; having all but attained it, they gave it away to the next generation. This process is repeated, less dramatically, in each individual and group of aging persons. The second image is of Jesus turning over his life, in mid-course, to a larger purpose and will. Not fully understanding yet believing in an unseen future, he gave his life away. This self-transcendence stands as the ideal of Christian maturity; it also describes an invitation within the process of psychosocial development.

THE MODES OF TRADITIONING VIRTUE

Adult growth, psychological and religious, happens best in community. Others teach us how to love and work well; our loved ones and fellow believers protect us during periods of crisis and assure us that we will survive. We have suggested that a function of a community is to structure rites of passage that will assist its members through the various transitions of growth. Between the traditional passages of marriage (most often at the beginning of adult life) and death (at its conclusion) lie the other significant challenges of adulthood. A faith community that is generative will find ways to facilitate its members through these often disguised passages. A central dynamic of such rites is to locate a person's distress within a larger pattern of suffering and growth, rescuing it from absurdity and idiosyncrasy. The exodus and exile of the Israelites, the passion, death, and resurrection of Jesus Christ function not as substitutes or distractions from an adult's distress but as signs that crisis and conflict can lead to growth. Further, they suggest that a person may *expect* to encounter God in these unlikely times.

The role of a faith community in its members' growth can be described in terms of four modes of traditioning virtue. "Traditioning" is used here to express the active part that a community and each adult Christian must play in handing on the faith. If we, as heirs, receive the Christian tradition in our childhood and youth, as generative adults we are called to hand on, to "tradition" to the next generation, what we have received.

The first mode of traditioning is that of inspiring. A community invokes the powerful metaphors and images of its tradition to call its members to the exercise of virtue. In preaching and other forms of religious rhetoric the Christian story is retold to believers, young and old, to excite them to similar action. This mode of traditioning fails when it becomes disengaged from the other modes of socialization or when the motivating metaphors of the tradition are not translated into contemporary images. When, for example, in a democratic and urban society Christian leadership is presented exclusively in images of kingship or of pastoring a flock, religious rhetoric easily becomes "rhetorical" in its most pejorative sense.

A second mode of transmitting virtue is educating. With its theology and moral education, a religious tradition instructs its members how to live. This educational mode outlines, more systematically than the previous mode, the parameters of the expression of Christian love and work in the world. This mode depends on and presents a working knowledge or "knowledge that facilitates behavior" (Egan and Cowan, 1979) of the human person and society. Such knowledge is borrowed by a religious tradition from the culture's understanding of human life (as earlier Christianity borrowed from and reinterpreted Aristotle). Today the Church is challenged to develop, especially in dialogue with psychology and sociology, more effective and compelling understandings of the person and society. We argue that this Christian interpretation must include a working knowledge of developmental change that will make more effective the Christian ministry to the challenges of adult growth. This mode of traditioning virtue fails when it is disengaged from the other modes and when "education" is believed to have a magical power of change. Knowledge is not yet virtue; educational formation must be complemented by other means of exciting persons to virtuous action.

A third mode of traditioning virtue is that of religious training. The knowledge and values handed on in education must be translated into one's actual behavior. In religious training one learns the particular skills that are necessary for effective religious living. Traditionally these skills principally focused on a person's relationship with God in the prayers and liturgical devotions learned informally in the home and more formally in the parochial school. A Catholic, for example, became more skilled at intimacy with God by repeated prayerful participation in the Eucharist, and more skilled in self-awareness and self-disclosure through the frequent experience of confession. Recent attention to the specific behavior involved in successful communication among persons and in effective helping relationships (Egan, 1975 and 1977) can suggest new possibilities for the training of adults in the virtues of Christian living. Skills of listening and self-disclosure, of assertion and conflict resolution can give concrete form to the Christian ideals concerning love and work.

A fourth mode of transmission is that of modeling. This occurs in a community as virtuous adults demonstrate behavior that is intimate, generative, and Christian. By witnessing effectively to the plural ways that the Christian virtues are lived, the community functions as a sacrament.[3] As a sacrament a community is a sign that Christian life is both possible and good. Further, it is a sign

3. The understanding of the Church as sacrament has received increasing attention recently. In *Lumen Gentium*, §1, the fathers of the Second Vatican Council recall, though somewhat hesitantly, that "the Church is a kind of sacrament. . . ." See also Semmelroth (1965) and Dulles (1974).

that effects more community—"see how they love one another" is both the acknowledgment of this sign and the beginning of an effort to emulate it.

Modeling is the context and foundation for the other modes of communicating virtue. When individual communities demonstrate to their young by modeling that Christian life is possible, that it is exciting and fruitful, its efforts to inspire, to educate, and to train are rescued from a sense of formalism, restraint, and ritualism and can become effective means of fostering religious development.

MATURITY: A FRAGILE STRENGTH

In our discussion of adulthood we have focused on the personal strengths and character resources that become available over the course of adult life. Maturing adults find themselves getting better at commitment, at caring for others, and at trusting in their own intuitions. We have stressed the active quality of these resources: Not only must they be exercised; they must remain open to modification and further development. But maturity is mutable from another direction as well. Adulthood is an unstable achievement, accompanied by both surprises and disappointments. Our maturity is built on the wounds and triumphs of earlier development. Unresolved conflicts and unhealed parts of our past return to disrupt our lives in the present. Maturity does not imply the absence of such conflicts and inconsistencies but the ability to accept this mosaic which is myself. Acceptance does not effect the transformation of these immaturities into health and wholeness; rather it reconciles me to the paradox of human maturity.

Over the course of life, in the successful resolution of each stage of adult development, an adult comes into possession of new and more adaptive abilities. In the exercise and development of these strengths over time, the resources can become habituated as virtues of one's personality. I can then come to count on my capacity to respond maturely. In this confidence, though, I retain the sense of how transient is my strength. With Paul, I know how often it is the things that I would not that I do (Rom. 7:15). This realization need not throw me into despair. It can be instead an impetus to patience with myself and to compassion for the failings of others. Maturity, then, includes an acceptance of lingering immaturity. "Full adulthood is not something permanent or ultimately triumphant," Sennett concludes; its full emotional strength "can be felt only as something fragile in time" (1970, p. 124).

Beyond cultural and religious expectations of adult maturity, each of us is invited to discover the meaning and shape of our own fragile maturity. In this discovery, which comes, as Erikson reminds us, "in moments of humor and wisdom, in prayer, meditation, and self-analysis," even our anxious worries about our own growth can themselves "be charitably transcended" (IR, p. 150).

LIFE BOUNDED BY DEATH

We have considered adult life chronologically, focusing in turn on each critical stage of development. But such a consideration is partial. Life is not lived simply as an unfolding into a boundless future. Human life is bounded by death. To be appreciated fully at any point in its course, life must be apprehended as a whole. Human life, then, must find its deepest meaning in its relation to death. But death seems to stand as a stubborn impediment to meaning. It destroys plans, it undercuts purpose, it breaks the bonds of love. Humankind has struggled to discern a meaning in life that can prevail against the power of death. In this struggle Christians have been among the most audacious. For we claim the hope of resurrection. This hope does not void death; death always precedes resurrection. For many of us it does not lessen death's difficulty or lighten its pain. But it rescues death from absurdity.

Jesus Christ stands for the Christian as the enduring witness to the promise of life through death. The religious conviction that arises from this promise finds resonance in the experience of loss and change in adult life. Growth does not come easily nor by simple addition. At each important junction in our life there is the threat of loss, the fear of what lies ahead, the temptation to hold on to what we already possess, and the resistance to standing open to the possibility of change and the ambiguity of a future that we do not control. Yet it has been through such experiences of confusion and loss that we have moved toward growth and fulfillment. It has been in letting go of the evanescent security of life under our own control that we have received the gifts of love and the true accomplishments that have enriched our life.

Hidden in the dynamic of adult growth is a confirmation of Christianity's deepest paradox. I must be willing to lose all in order to find myself. It is in letting go of life that I discover it. And in dying, we believe, we shall find life.

References

Biblical quotations are from *The Oxford Annotated Bible*. Revised Standard Version. New York: Oxford University Press, 1977.

Anciaux, Paul. *The Sacrament of Penance*. New York: Sheed and Ward, 1962.

Anderson, Bernard. *Understanding the Old Testament*. 3rd ed. Englewood Cliffs, N.J.: Prentice-Hall, 1975.

Barr, James. *Biblical Words for Time*. Naperville, Ill.: Alec R. Allenson, Inc., 1962.

Baum, Gregory. "Catholic Homosexuals." *Commonweal*, 99 (1974): 479–82.

Benedek, T. "Parenthood as a Developmental Phase." *Journal of the American Psychoanalytic Association*, 7 (1959): 389–417.

Blank, Josef. *Krisis*. Freiburg im Breisgau: Lambertus Verlag, 1964.

Bornkamm, Gunther. *Paul*. New York: Harper Row, 1971.

Bortner, R. W., and D. F. Hultsch. "Personal Time Perspective in Adulthood." *Developmental Psychology*, 7 (1972): 98–103.

Boulding, Kenneth. *The Image: Knowledge in Life and Society*. Ann Arbor: University of Michigan Press, 1956.

Bouwsma, William. "Christian Adulthood." *Daedalus*, 105 (1976): 77–92.

Browning, Don. *Generative Man: Psychoanalytic Perspectives*. Philadelphia: Westminster, 1973.

Burghardt, Walter. *Towards Reconciliation*. Washington, D.C.: United States Catholic Conference, 1974.

Butler, Robert N. "The Life Review: An Interpretation of Reminiscence in the Aged." In Bernice Neugarten, ed., *Middle Age and Aging*, pp. 486–96. Chicago: University of Chicago Press, 1968.

Callahan, Sidney, and Drew Christiansen. "Ideal Old Age." *Soundings*, 57 (1974): 1–16.

Clines, David. "Sin and Maturity." *Journal of Psychology and Theology*, 5 (1977): 183–96.

Coles, Robert. "Creativity, Leadership and Psychohistory." In *The Mind's Fate*, pp. 161–272. Boston: Little, Brown, 1966.

Crossan, John Dominic. *The Dark Interval: Towards a Theology of Story*. Chicago: Argus, 1975.

Douglas, Mary. *Purity and Danger: An Analysis of Concepts of Pollution and Taboo*. London: Routledge and Kegan Paul, 1966.

Driver, Tom F. "Speaking from the Body." In John Y. Fenton, ed., *Theology and Body*, pp. 100–26. Philadelphia: Westminster, 1974.

Dulles, Avery. *Models of the Church*. New York: Doubleday, 1974.

Egan, Gerard. "Ministering Community and Community of Ministers." In Evelyn Eaton Whitehead, ed., *The Parish in Community and Ministry*. New York: Paulist, 1978.

——. *The Skilled Helper*. Monterey, Calif.: Brooks/Cole, 1975.

——. *You and Me*. Monterey, Calif.: Brooks/Cole, 1977.

——, and Michael Cowan. *People in Systems*. Monterey, Calif.: Brooks/Cole, 1979.

Eliade, Mircea. *Patterns in Comparative Religion*. New York: Sheed and Ward, 1958.

Erikson, Erik H. *Childhood and Society*. 2nd ed. New York: Norton 1963. Cited in the text as CS.

——. "Dr. Borg's Life-Cycle." *Daedalus*, 105 (1976): 1–28. This issue of *Daedalus* has been reissued, under Erikson's editorship, as *Adulthood*. New York: Norton, 1978. Cited as DBL.

——. "Identity and the Life-Cycle." *Psychological Issues*, vol. 1. New York: International Universities Press, 1959. Cited as ILC.

——. *Identity: Youth and Crisis*. New York: Norton, 1968. Cited as IYC.

——. *Insight and Responsibility*. New York: Norton, 1964. Cited as IR.

——. *Young Man Luther*. New York: Norton, 1962. Cited as YML.

Goergen, Donald. *The Sexual Celibate*. New York: Seabury, 1974.

Goldbrunner, Josef. *Holiness Is Wholeness*. Notre Dame, Ind.: University of Notre Dame Press, 1964.

Gorer, Geoffrey. *Death, Grief and Mourning in Contemporary Britain*. London: Cresset Press, 1965.

Gould, Roger. "The Phases of Adult Life: A Study in Developmental Psychology." *American Journal of Psychiatry*, 129 (1972): 33–43.

Greenleaf, Robert K. *Servant Leadership*. New York: Paulist, 1977.

Hansell, Norris. "Managing People Through Crises." *Innovation*, 22 (1971): 2–11.

——, Mary Wodarczyk, and Britemar Handlon-Lathrop. "Decision Counseling Method: Expanding Coping at Crisis-in-Transit." *Archives of General Psychiatry*, 22 (1970): 462–67.

Hauerwas, Stanley. *Character and the Christian Life: A Study in Theological Ethics.* San Antonio: Trinity University Press, 1975.

Havighurst, Robert. *Human Development and Education.* New York: Longman, 1953.

——. "Successful Aging." *The Gerontologist,* 1 (1961): 1–13.

Hellwig, Monika. *The Meaning of the Sacraments.* Dayton, Ohio: Pflaum, 1972.

Henry, Patrick. "Homosexuals: Identity and Dignity." *Theology Today,* 33 (1976): 33–39.

Jahoda, Marie. *Current Concepts of Positive Mental Health.* New York: Basic Books, 1959.

Jaques, Elliot. "Death and the Mid-Life Crisis." In Hendrik M. Ruitenbeek, ed., *The Interpretation of Death,* pp. 140–65. New York: Jason Aronson, 1973.

Jaspert, Bernd. "'Krisis' als kirchengeschichtliche Kategorie." In Bernd Jaspert and Rudolph Mohn, eds., *Traditio–Krisis–Renovatio aus theologischer Sicht,* pp. 24–40. Marburg: N. G. Elwert Verlag, 1976.

Jung, Carl. *Man and His Symbols.* New York: Doubleday, 1964.

Kelleher, Stephen J. *Divorce and Remarriage for Catholics?* New York: Doubleday, 1976.

Léon-Dufour, Xavier. *Dictionary of Biblical Theology.* New York: Seabury, 1967.

Levinson, Daniel. *The Seasons of a Man's Life.* New York: Knopf, 1978.

Linn, Matthew, and Dennis Linn. *Healing of Memories.* New York: Paulist, 1974.

Lowenthal, Marjorie Fiske, and David Chiriboga. "Transition to the Empty Nest: Crisis, Challenge, or Relief?" *Archives of General Psychiatry,* 26 (1972): 8–14.

Lowenthal, Marjorie Fiske, Majda Thurnher, and David Chiriboga. *Four Stages of Life.* San Francisco: Jossey-Bass, 1976.

Lumen Gentium: The Dogmatic Constitution on the Church. In Walter M. Abbott, ed., *Documents of Vatican II.* New York: America Press, 1966, pp. 14–101.

McKenzie, John L. *Dictionary of the Bible.* Milwaukee: Bruce, 1965.

McNeill, John. *The Church and the Homosexual.* Kansas City: Sheed Andrews and McMeel, 1976.

Marris, Peter. *Loss and Change.* New York: Doubleday, 1975.

Mencius. *The Works of Mencius.* Translated and edited by James Legge. New York: Dover, 1970.

National Council on Aging. *The Myth and Reality of Aging in America.* Washington, D.C.: NCOA, 1975.

Neugarten, Bernice. "Adaptation and the Life Cycle." *Journal of Geriatric Psychiatry*, 4 (1970): 71–87.

——. "The Future of the Young-Old." *The Gerontologist*, 15 (1975), no. 1, part 2, pp. 4–9.

——, ed. *Middle Age and Aging*. Chicago: University of Chicago Press, 1968.

Noonan, John T. *The Power to Dissolve*. Cambridge, Mass.: Harvard University Press, 1972.

Nouwen, Henry J. M. "The Self-Availability of the Homosexual." In W. Dwight Oberholtzer, ed., *Is Gay Good?*, pp. 204–12. Philadelphia: Westminster, 1971.

Progoff, Ira. *At a Journal Workshop*. New York: Dialogue House, 1975.

Rahner, Karl. "Grace." In *Sacramentum Mundi: An Encyclopedia of Theology*, vol. 2, pp. 409–24. New York: Herder and Herder, 1968.

Riley, Matilda White, et al. *Aging and Society*. Vol. 3, *A Sociology of Age Stratification*. New York: Russell Sage, 1970.

Rite of Penance, The. Collegeville, Minn.: Liturgical Press, 1975.

Schweizer, Eduard. *Lordship and Discipleship*. London: SCM Press, 1960.

Semmelroth, O. *Church and Sacrament*. Notre Dame, Ind.: Fides, 1965.

Sennett, Richard. *The Uses of Disorder: Personal Identity and City Life*. New York: Vintage, 1970.

Seper, Cardinal Franjo. Signator of *Declaration on the Question of the Admission of Women to the Ministerial Priesthood*. Washington, D.C.: USCC, 1977.

Sheehy, Gail. *Passages: Predictable Crises of Adult Life*. New York: Dutton, 1976.

Sumiya, Kazuhiko. "The Long March and the Exodus." In Bruce Douglas and Ross Terrill, eds., *China and Ourselves*. Boston: Beacon Press, 1969.

Tillich, Paul. *The Interpretation of History*. New York: Scribner, 1936.

Tournier, Paul. *Learn to Grow Old*. Translated by Edwin Hudson. New York: Harper Row, 1972.

Turner, Victor. "Passages, Margins, and Poverty: Religious Symbols of Communitas." *Worship*, 46 (1972): 390–412, 482–94.

——. *The Ritual Process*. New York: Cornell University Press, 1969.

Vaillant, George E. *Adaptation to Life*. Boston: Little, Brown, 1977.

Van Gennep, Arnold. *The Rites of Passage*. Translated by Monika B. Vizedom and Gabrielle L. Caffee. Chicago: University of Chicago Press, 1960. (*Les Rites de Passage*. Paris: E. Nourry, 1908.)

Von Rad, Gerhard. *Genesis: A Commentary.* Translated by John H. Marks. Philadelphia: Westminster, 1961.

White, Robert W. *Lives in Progress: A Study of the Natural Growth of Personality.* 3rd ed. New York: Holt, Rinehart and Winston, 1975.

Zullo, James. *Mid-Life: Crisis of Limits.* N.C.R. Cassettes. Kansas City, Mo.: National Catholic Reporter, 1977.

Index

Aaron, 65
Abraham, 17
Acceptance, self-. *See* Intimacy;
    specific stages
Acts of the Apostles, 59 n, 60 n,
    67 n, 146 n
Adolescence (teen-agers), 31, 37, 42,
    51, 62, 63, 74, 75, 79, 113, 119,
    126, 196; second, 129; and time
    distortion, 66
Age, 51 n. *See also* Time; specific
    stages
Aggressiveness, 129. *See also* Asser-
    tiveness
Aging. *See* Mature adulthood
Agricultural (nature) metaphors,
    14–16, 40 n
Ambivalence, 53–54
Amos, 67
Anamnesis, 185–87
Anciaux, Paul, 146 n
Anderson, Bernard, 65 n
Androgyny, 131–32, 143
Anger, 129
Annulment, 100
Apprenticeship, 139
Architectural metaphor, 39–40
Aristotle, 200
Asceticism, 36
Assertiveness (assertion), 94, 95,
    123, 130
Attachment/separateness. *See* Polari-
    ties
Avoidance, 85–86
Awareness, self-, 94, 95. *See also* Inti-
    macy; specific stages

Baptism, 34–35, 146, 186, 187
Barr, James, 67 n, 68 n
Barron, Frank, 20 n
Barth, Karl, 35
Baum, Gregory, 106 n
Benedek, T., 108
Bethlehem, star of, 67 n
Bible, 136. *See also* specific books
Birth, 62
Blank, Josef, 58 n
Bornkamm, Gunther, 40 n, 59 n,
    60 n
Bortner, R. W., 66
Boulding, Kenneth, 27
Bouwsma, William, 36–37
Browning, Don, 42, 87, 108, 149–50
Buhler, Charlotte, 19
Burghardt, Walter, 146 n
Burrell, David, 138 n–39 n
Butler, Robert N., 185–86

Callahan, Sidney, 182
Calvin, John, 37
Care, 32, 33, 42, 114, 118, 119–24.
    See also Generativity
Career. *See* Work
Catholics. *See* Roman Catholics
Celibacy, 79–80, 152–53
Change, 25–46 (*See also* Crises;
    specific stages); Christianity and
    personal, 34–40; Christian virtue,
    psychological strength, personal
    skill, 41–45; critical stages, 30–34
    (*See also* Crises; specific stages);
    perspectives of Erik Erikson,

28–30; psychology and personal, 27–28

Charity, 43, 151

Children, 37–38, 84, 108, 113, 119 ff., 137, 149, 159, 167, 171, 193 (*See also* Adolescence); ambitions of, 115; death of, 51; grandparents and baptism, 186; imagery and development of, 16

China, 151–52

Chiriboga, David, 125 n

Choices, 195–97

Christiansen, Drew, 182

Chronos, 67–70

Clergy, 37 n, 137–38

Clines, David, 38 n

Coles, Robert, 107

Colossians, 40 n, 146 n

Combative relationships, 75

"Coming out," 96, 103–6

Command, metaphor of, 35, 36

Commitment, 43, 100. *See also* Generativity; Marriage; Middle adulthood

Communes, 195 n

Communication, 95, 200

Community, 56–58 (*See also* specific stages); and traditioning virtue, 198–201

Competition, 75, 80–81, 82, 86, 192

Concern. *See* Generativity

Confession, 109, 144, 200

Confrontation, 43–44

Control, 148–49. *See also* Middle adulthood

Conversion, 34–37. *See also* Paul, St.

Co-operation (collaboration), 75, 76, 80–81, 82, 86 ff.

Corinthians: I, 15, 136, 146 n; II, 35, 37 ff., 145, 179

Cowan, Michael, 43, 199

Creativity, 17, 83, 116, 118 ff., 148. *See also* Generativity; Polarities

Crises, 17, 30–34, 47–70 (*See also* Change; specific stages); dynamic of, 53–56; exodus, 64–66; and experience of time, 66–70; as religious event, 58–62; as religious

passage, 62–64; role of community, 56–58; structure of, 50–53

Crossan, John Dominic, 192, 194–95

Dating, 86

Death, 18, 50, 51, 57, 60, 62, 97, 113, 119, 125–26, 129, 158, 159, 163 ff., 171, 175, 177, 186, 194, 196, 199 (*See also* Loss; Mature adulthood; Rebirth); integrity and, 167–68; life bounded by, 202–3; sacrament of the dying, 146, 187

Dependence, 120, 124, 183–84. *See also* Children; Generativity

Despair, 31 ff., 160, 161, 163–64, 165

Destructiveness. *See* Polarities

Detachment, 151

Development, growth as, 14. *See also* Change

Diakonia, 136–38

Dignity (organization), 105

Diminishment. *See* Mature adulthood

Discipleship, 138–43

Disgust, 160, 164

Disorientation, 53, 65

Divorce, 50, 51, 53, 63, 93, 96–103

Douglas, Mary, 54, 64

Dream, the, 116 ff., 126, 127–28, 130, 136, 141, 144 ff., 195, 196

Driver, Tom, 109

Dulles, Avery, 200 n

Easter, 186

Edification, 39–40

Education, 94, 144, 199–200

Egan, Gerard, 23, 43, 95, 138, 199, 200

"Ego strengths," 33

Eliade, Mircea, 67 n

Elizabeth (mother of John the Baptist), 67

Empathy, 43–44, 83, 84, 198

Emptying, 61, 181–82, 188–89. *See also* Letting go

"Empty nest," 125

"End-time," 59, 68. *See also* Crises

Ephesians, 36 ff., 146 n
Episcopal group for homosexuals, 105
Erikson, Erik, *passim*
Eucharist, 108, 147, 175, 186, 200
Evil, 16
Exodus, 20, 64–66

Failure, 17–18. See also Polarities;
    specific stages
Faithfulness. See Commitment; Fi-
    delity
Families. See Children; Generativity;
    Middle adulthood
Femininity/masculinity. See Polari-
    ties
Fidelity, 42, 91, 100. See also Com-
    mitment; Generativity; Loyalty
Fifties. See Middle adulthood
Flexibility, 83, 84
Forgiveness, 109, 142, 145, 162
Forties, 109. See also Middle adult-
    hood
Friendship, 75, 76–77, 82–84, 86, 88

Galatians, 38 n, 59 n, 143, 179
Games, 192
Gays. See Homosexuality
Generativity, 17, 31 ff., 41 ff., 45, 49,
    50, 87, 113, 116 ff., 170, 171, 198,
    199 (See also Middle adulthood);
    challenge of, 119–24; *diakonia* and
    Christian ministry, 136–38; from
    discipleship to stewardship,
    138–43; and leadership, 131–32,
    135; and leaving an "afterwards,"
    151–53; religious, 133–53; religious
    dimensions of mid-life passage,
    140–43; rites of reconciliation,
    143–47; successful and unsuccess-
    ful passage, 147–51
Genesis, 15, 42, 91
Gennep. See Van Gennep, Arnold
Goergen, Donald, 106 n
Goldbrunner, Josef, 20
Gorer, Geoffrey, 57
Gospels, 138 n. See also specific Gos-
    pels
Gould, Roger, 108

Grace, 16–17, 20, 21, 37
Greenleaf, Robert K., 138
Grieving (grief), 56, 59. See also
    Death; Loss
Guilt, 97, 109, 129, 142

Hansell, Norris, 52 n ff., 57
Harlotry, 99
Harvard University, 19
Hauerwas, Stanley, 35
Havighurst, Robert, 19, 159
Healing, 109, 136, 142. See also
    past; reconciliation
Health, 18–21. See also Mature
    adulthood
Hebrews, 58. See also Exodus; Israel
Hellwig, Monika, 146 n
Henry, Patrick, 106 n
Homosexuality, 79; "coming out,"
    96, 103–6
Hosea, 67 n, 99
Hultsh, D. F., 66
Humanism, 194

Identity, 93. See also Young adult-
    hood
Ignatius Loyola, 136
Illness. See Health
Illusions, 126. See also Dream, the
Images (metaphors), 14–18, 27, 199.
    See also specific stages
Imagination, 130
Incorporation, 63, 64
Independence, 31. See also Depend-
    ence; Young adulthood
Infants, 38, 197
Inspiration, 75, 81–82, 199
Integrity, 31, 33, 42, 45, 49, 50,
    161–68 ff., 177, 179, 180, 197. See
    also Mature adulthood
Integrity (organization), 105
Interiority, 114, 124–30, 141, 142,
    159. See also Mature adulthood;
    Middle adulthood
Intimacy, 31 ff., 41, 45, 49, 50, 66,
    71–109, 115 ff., 120, 125, 166,
    193, 196, 197 (See also Love;
    Work); disguised passages of,

96–106; failure of, 85–86; and love, 86–88; and religious growth, 89–109; self-, 106–9; sexuality and, 73–75; social contexts of, 75–82; strengths of, 82–85
Intuition, 75, 81–82
Isaac, 15, 17
Isaiah, 137
Isolation, 31, 53, 84, 85–86, 87, 101
Israel, 67, 99, 100

Jacob, 91–92
Jaques, Elliot, 125 n
Jaspert, Bernd, 58 n
Jerome, St., 36
Jesus Christ, 18, 39, 43, 59 ff., 67, 68, 108, 135, 137 ff., 143, 175, 182, 186, 198, 199, 202; and conversion, 34; and Sabbath, 38; truncated growth, 17
Jews. *See* Hebrews; Israel
Jobs. *See* Work
John, Book of, 40 n, 58 n, 61, 68, 136 n, 137, 139, 192
John the Baptist, 34, 40 n, 67 n
Judges, 65
Jungian theory, 128

Kairos, 67–70
Kelleher, Stephen J., 98
Kris, Ernst, 108

Late adulthood. *See* Mature adulthood
Leadership, 131–32, 135. *See also* Generativity; Middle adulthood
Legge, James, 151 n
Léon-Dufour, Xavier, 42, 67 n
Letting go, 55, 97, 148–49, 165, 192–95, 198, 202–3. *See also* Emptying
Levinson, Daniel, 19, 22, 66, 79, 113 ff., 119, 125, 127, 128, 131, 137, 141, 142
Life expectancy, 12
"Life review," 185–87
Linn, Matthew and Dennis, 109
Listening, 94, 95

Loss (losing), 18, 49 n, 50, 53 ff., 59 ff., 181–83, 192, 194. *See also* Death; Intimacy; Letting go
Love (loving), 18, 31 ff., 41, 43–44, 76, 86–88, 109 n, 126, 162, 166, 191 ff., 195 ff. *See also* Intimacy; Mentors; Sexuality; specific stages
Lowenthal, Marjorie Fiske, 19, 22, 114, 117, 125
Loyalty, 83, 84. *See also* Commitment; Fidelity
Luke, 37, 39, 60, 67 n, 68, 135, 139 n, 140 n, 186
Luther, Martin, 39, 55, 136

McKenzie, John L., 68
McNeil, John, 106 n
Mark, 34, 37, 40 n, 60 n, 67, 68, 135 n
Marriage (matrimony), 13, 51–52, 53, 62, 77–80, 87–88, 91, 98, 115 n, 116, 127, 187, 199 (*See also* Divorce); as religious passage of intimacy, 93–96
Marris, Peter, 49 n, 52 n, 53, 56, 66, 97
Marsh, Barr's critique of, 67 n
Masculinity/femininity. *See* Polarities
Matthew, 37 ff., 58 n, 60, 67, 135, 140 n, 146 n, 192
Mature adulthood (late adulthood), 31, 32, 155–90, 194; aging in cultural context, 168–71; challenge of, 158–61; Christian meaning in, 176–83; contributions to community, 183–85; growing old among Christians, 173–90; integrity and death, 167–68; integrity and despair, 163–64; integrity the strength of, 161–63; the past and *anamnesis*, 185–87; sacrament of aging, 187–90; wisdom the fruit of integrity, 164–67
Meaning of life. *See* Mature adulthood
Memories. *See* Past
Mencius, 15, 151–52
Menopause, 51, 125

Mentors, 116–17, 118, 130, 131,
    137, 139
Metaphors (images), 14–18, 27, 199.
    See also specific stages
Middle adulthood (mid-years), 31,
    111–32, 59, 163, 165, 167, 170,
    193–94 ff. (*See also* Generativity);
    challenge of generative care,
    119–24; experience of, 118–19; in-
    teriority and mid-life transition,
    124–32; personal power, 115–18;
    psychological issues, 114
"Mid-life transition" (crisis; passage),
    66, 124–30, 140–43, 196–97
Ministry. *See* Clergy; Generativity
Mobility, 12–13
Modeling, 200–1
Moses, 20, 64, 198
Mourning. *See* Death; Grieving
Mutuality. *See* Young adulthood
Myers, J. Gordon, 49 n
Myth vs. parable, 194–95

National Council on Aging, 157
Nature, 14–17, 20
Need. *See* Dependence
Neugarten, Bernice L., 19, 22, 51,
    96, 114, 119, 124, 125 n, 158
Noonan, John T., 98
North American Conference of Sepa-
    rated and Divorced Catholics, 98 n
Nouwen, Henry J. M., 104
"Nuclear conflict," 33
Numbers, Book of, 65

O'Brien, David, 138 n
Occupation. *See* Work
Old age. *See* Mature adulthood;
    Mentors
Ordination, 187
Orgasm, 75, 77, 84

Parable vs. myth, 194–95
Parents, 51, 84, 108, 113, 119 ff.,
    159. *See also* Children; Genera-
    tivity
Particularity, 195–97

Passage. *See* Crises; Rites; specific
    stages
Passivity, 55, 64, 65, 87
Past, 7–9, 10, 119, 142, 159, 161,
    185–87. *See also* Forgiveness
Pastors, 137–38
Paul, St. (Pauline writings),
    36–37 ff., 59–60, 136, 145–46
    (*See also* specific Epistles); and
    imagery, 15, 16
Penance, 109, 144, 146
Philippians, 36, 61 n, 182
Piaget, Browning uses distinction of
    work and play of, 150 n
Play, 130, 149–50
Pluralism, 180, 197
Polarities, 128–30, 131–32, 141,
    142–43, 147 ff.
Power, 41–46, 114, 115–18. *See also*
    Generativity; specific stages
Prayer, 142, 200
Preaching, 199
Prevailing, 92, 192
Productivity, 116, 118 ff., 148. *See*
    also Work
Progoff, Ira, 23
Promiscuity, 85
Psalms, 137

Rahner, Karl, 17 n
Rebirth, 34–35, 36
Reconciliation, 101, 109, 141, 142,
    143–47, 196. *See also* Polarities
Reflection, 22–23, 142. *See also*
    specific stages
Remarriage, 99
Renunciation, 181–83. *See also* Let-
    ting go
Repentance. *See* Conversion
Responsibility, 97, 114, 118 ff., 131,
    160. *See also* Care; Generativity
Resurrection, 175
Retirement, 50, 51, 158, 178,
    187–88
Revelation, 175
Riley, Matilda White, 51 n

Rites, 57–58, 62 ff., 143–44, 199. *See also* specific crises, rites, stages
Ritual, 143, 144. *See also* Rites
Robinson, J. A. T., 67 n
Roman Catholics, 17, 37 n, 147, 200 (*See also* specific rites); and divorce, 98–100; organization for gays, 105
Romans, Epistle to, 16, 37, 38 n, 39, 68, 145, 146, 201

Sabbath, 67
Sacraments. *See* Rites; specific sacraments
Saints, 20
Samuel II, 20
Sarah (Abraham's wife), 17
Schweizer, Eduard, 139 n
Second Vatican Council, 200 n
Self, 83, 84 (*See also* Intimacy; Intuition; specific aspects, stages); -centeredness, 31; -expression (*See* Young adulthood); -worth, basis of, 177–79
Semmelroth, O., 200 n
Sennett, Richard, 22, 54, 123, 202
Separateness/attachment. *See* Polarities
Separation, 63
Service, 43, 135. *See also* Generativity
Sexuality, 73–75, 76, 77–80, 84, 86, 91, 149, 198. *See also* Homosexuality; Love; Polarities
Sharing, 43–44
Sheehy, Gail, 19
Shepherd, image of, 137
Sin, 16, 17, 37–39, 146
Sinai, Mount, 65
Skills, 41–45, 94–95, 200
Society. *See* specific stages
Solidarity, group, 75, 76–77
Song of Solomon, 91
Sports, 81, 192
Stanislaus, St., 17
Stereotyped behavior (stereotyping), 85, 86, 103
Stewardship, 138–43

Strength, 41–45. *See also* Power; specific stages
Sumiya, Kazuhiko, 64 n

Teen-agers. *See* Adolescence
Thessalonians, 39, 67 n
Thirties. *See* Middle adulthood
Tillich, Paul, 68
Time, 119, 125, 129, 164 (*See also* Past); crisis, passage, and, 66–70
Timothy II, 185
Tolerance, 83
Tradition, 148–49, 198–201
Training, religious, 200
Transcendence, self-, 197–201. *See also* Generativity; Mature adulthood
Transition, 63
Trust, 150
Turner, Victor, 62–63, 64
Twenties, 51–52. *See also* Young adulthood

Vaillant, George, 19 ff., 66, 79, 113, 114, 119, 124 ff., 129 n, 131, 137, 150, 152 n, 195 n
Van Gennep, Arnold, 62, 63
Virtue, Christian, 41–45
Vision, Christian, 136–37
Vocation, 141–42. *See also* Dream, the
Von Rad, Gerhard, 91, 92

White, Robert, 15–16
Widowhood, 51
Wisdom, 32, 33, 42, 164–67, 170, 175, 189
Wisdom, Book of, 17
Women, 119, 125, 128 (*See also* Divorce; Marriage); and mentors, 117
Work (career; job; occupation), 18, 50, 51, 53, 113 ff., 121, 125, 126, 128, 130, 131, 140, 141, 148, 166, 167, 178, 191 ff. (*See also* Retirement); and play, 149–50

Yahweh, 20, 64 ff., 99, 100, 198

Yale Univresity, 19   "Young-old," the 158
Young, James, 98 n   Young v. old. *See* Polarities
Young adulthood, 31 ff., 43, 71–88,
   115 ff., 119, 126, 127, 130, 139, 195,
   197. *See also* Dream, the; Intimacy   Zullo, James, 125

Notes on the Authors

Evelyn Eaton Whitehead is a developmental psychologist (Ph.D., University of Chicago) who writes and lectures on adult maturity, the dynamics of leadership, and the social analysis of community and parish life. *James D. Whitehead* is a pastoral theologian and historian of religion (Ph.D., Harvard University) concerned with issues of contemporary spirituality, ministerial leadership, and theological method in ministry.

The Whiteheads are consultants in education and ministry through Whitehead Associates, which they established in 1978. Their ministry serves dioceses and religious congregations in the U.S. and internationally, contributing to programs of ministry education, leadership development, and adult formation in faith.

They have co-authored several books, the most recent of which is *The Promise of Partnership: Leadership and Ministry in an Adult Church* (Harper San Francisco, 1991).

Other books by the Whiteheads include:

A Sense of Sexuality: Christian Love and Intimacy. Image Books/Doubleday, 1990. A selection of Clergy Book Service. Book-of-the-Year Award, *Human Development* Magazine.

Christian Life Patterns. New York: Crossroad, 1992. Reprint Edition. A selection of the Catholic Book Club.

Community of Faith: Crafting Christian Communities Today. Mystic, CT: Twenty-Third Publications, 1992.

The Emerging Laity: Returning Leadership to the Community of Faith. Image Books/Doubleday, 1988. A selection of the Clergy Book Service.

Seasons of Strength: New Visions of Adult Christian Maturing. Image Books/Doubleday, 1986.

Method in Ministry: Theological Reflection and Christian Ministry. Harper & Row, 1979.

Marrying Well: Stages on the Journey of Christian Marriage. Image Books/Doubleday, 1983. A selection of the Religious Book Club.

The Whiteheads are Associate Faculty of the Institute of Pastoral Studies at Loyola University of Chicago, with which they have been affiliated since 1970. In fall 1992 they will serve as Distinguished Visiting Professors at the Warren Center for Catholic Studies at the University of Tulsa. From 1973–78 they were members of the graduate theological faculty at the University of Notre Dame. The Whiteheads currently make their home in South Bend, Indiana.

WHITEHEAD ASSOCIATES   19120 OAKMONT   SOUTH BEND, IN 46637